Code 10-71

Victim to Victor
A True Story

Madeline Morehouse

Code 10-71

Victim to Victor

A True Story

ISBN: 1533179042

ISBN-13: 978-1533179043

DEDICATION

For Jeffery Morehouse and Michelle Morehouse-D'Onofrio.
My grandchildren Evan, Mackenzie, Mochi, Milana and Vinny and
to all victims of violence who continue to suffer.

Code 10-71

ACKNOWLEDGMENTS

As a distinguished editor and friend from Dana Point, California, Tanya Besmehn, along with her gifted and extraordinary talent and skill brought my story to completion. I am forever grateful and blessed.

It's impossible to thank all those who touched my life during my journey to a place of healing, but I feel compelled to express my heartfelt thanks to Detective Jeff Jones, Edmonds, WA and Detective Joe Bruce, Lynnwood, WA. Officer L. P. Miller and Sgt. Debbie Smith, Edmonds Police Department.

A very special thanks to my children who were ever present and took over when I needed them most. My forever friends Kim Pearson Bacon and Renee M. Schumacher, Mike Santopolo, who so kindly offered his home as a central meeting point. I will never forget the kindness of Cindy and Scott Abrahamson. My physician, Dr. Les Newton, counselors Dr. Gregory Jantz and Dr. Ginnet Perrin.

CHAPTER 1 – HEALING CASSIE

"Time heals all wounds. But not this one. Not yet."
~ Marie Lu

Girls with black eyes don't wear mascara. They don't wear lipstick either. In fact, the only thing I ever noticed was the excessive use of concealer; her way of telling the rest of the world that, although they found her as riveting as a fatality on the freeway, she was actually quite fine and, while stuck in a quicksand of hell, would very much like for them to move on. That there was really nothing to see here.

Girls with six-inch multi-colored bruises along their rib cage don't wear crop tops. They give no chance peek to the passerby who might determine she was violated to the point that her body felt more like the enemy now and deserved no attempts at a parade down Main Street for all to appreciate, envy or emulate. Gone too are the trendy heels, now replaced with cheap flip-flops that allowed her toes to heal. Those same toes that cracked and crumbled from the blunt force to her attacker's kneecap over and over and over again.

Cassie Haden sat across from me while I took silent inventory of what a rape victim does and doesn't expose, she looked a lot older than her nineteen years and I wondered how much of that was due to the events of the previous February. It had been a long day and I was having trouble staying focused on her words.

She had mentioned for the fourth time how her attacker's breath smelled of a nauseating mix of Juicy Fruit gum and stale tobacco; that she was angry because she had once enjoyed Juicy Fruit and now the thought of it, never mind the smell and taste, made her gag. She may have needed to mention the gum a fourth time, but it was my job as her rape counselor to listen all four times – and a fifth when she deemed necessary.

Cassie worked at a mini-mart on the outskirts of Tacoma, the kind of place one stopped to fill up the tank and pick up a quart of milk to see the family to the weekly grocery stock-up. She worked the four-midnight shift so she could spend the bulk of the day with her two-year old son, Trevor, before leaving him with her mom, Donna, and step-dad, Brian.

Cassie's own father had left just shy of her sixth birthday. He'd telephone from time to time and would occasionally send a gift at Christmas or on her birthday, but once she'd entered middle-school the calls and packages all but stopped. He had a new family near Spokane and had left his former life well in his wake. Trevor's dad, Josh, had graduated from high-school and after a summer of avoiding Cassie, headed to a resort in Steamboat Springs to become a ski instructor three months before Trevor was born. Cassie left school in December of her senior year to give birth and never looked back.

Cassie's relationship with Brian had quickly deteriorated when he learned of her pregnancy, he'd constantly shake his head and roll his eyes to friends and neighbors saying, "She went and got herself pregnant." Cassie found that statement to be less an idiom and more idiotic, placing the blame squarely on her shoulders and releasing Josh from any responsibility toward her, or his son. Josh had offered to pay for an abortion, but Cassie refused, not for any moral reasons, she just had a strong feeling about the baby. While Elle stood by her daughter's decision, Brian was convinced she was ruining her life and made a point of constantly reminding her of that fact. It seemed men had a way of disappointing her.

It was eleven-thirty on that fateful February night, Cassie was thumbing through the latest issue of Glamour Magazine when an '87 Ford Taurus with California plates pulled to the pump. She remembers thinking how strange it was for someone to leave the sun and sand of California for the sloppy-slippery streets of Tacoma in February. He walked in and threw a ten-dollar bill on the counter, "Ten on two," he said. His voice was a touch hoarse, like he had chain-smoked his way up the coast and Cassie found something disquieting about him.

"Long way from home," she said, trying to make small-talk. His eyes scanned Cassie from the top of her head to where her jeans disappeared behind the counter, a barrier Cassie suddenly felt grateful for. He picked up a pack of Juicy Fruit and fished in his pocket for a quarter which he tossed on the counter. "Yep," he said, then turned and left. Cassie was glad when he pumped his gas and drove out of the lot.

It was close to midnight when Cassie took a walk around the store to ensure everything was in order. She straightened shelves, threw away candy wrappers the local kids carelessly tossed to the floor on their way out the door and stepped into the back office to hit the pump lights and grab her purse. As she reached for her jacket, the office door closed and there stood the man with the California plates.

Cassie tried to stay calm, but was sure he could see her hands begin to shake, "You forget something?" She asked.

"I did," he said. She remembers the creepy smile which revealed a gap where the left front tooth should have been.

She moved to the door, "Well, let me just get to my —", she never finished her sentence. He grabbed her around the waist, picked her small frame up with ease, slammed her against the wall and raped her for the next hour.

When Cassie's mother awoke to Travis' cries at 3a.m., she checked Cassie's room and found her bed empty. She woke Brian and begged him to go and check the station, claiming there was no way Cassie would shirk her responsibility to Trevor. She was always home by 12:20am, at the latest—she knew she had less than six hours before Trevor would be hungry for breakfast and made a point of getting every moment of precious sleep she could.

Brian found the station unlocked, the cash drawer open and empty and Cassie crouched in the corner of the office, she was bruised, shaking and in shock. His first words to his step-daughter were, "For God's sake, Cassie! Now what have you done?"

* * * *

Cassie continued seeing me every Thursday afternoon since late February and now, three months later, I felt she was ready to reclaim the rest of her life. Her visible bruises had long since faded. She had registered for the upcoming summer classes to obtain her GED and had plans to work at a daycare in town where she could bring Trevor for free until he would be ready for pre-school. This would ensure she could be home every evening and still spend time with her son. She never returned to the mini-mart and made a point of using any alternate route to avoid driving by the place.

She and Trevor moved into an apartment over her mother's garage and Brian, who had taken a workshop in sensitivity at Elle's prodding, equipped the space with an alarm system that would sound in the main house, as well as her apartment, if anyone so much as wiggled the doorknob. It gave her a sense of security, and she would need that for quite some time to come.

The man from California was never found and while Cassie remembered it was an '87 Taurus, she really couldn't tell you if it were black, grey or navy blue. That didn't help the police and they quickly wrote him off as a stranger driving through town, they had DNA evidence and promised Cassie they'd keep a watchful eye in the event he showed up on his way back to California.

It was our first meeting in May and I told Cassie that since there was no trial, I felt the best thing for her was to put the experience behind her. Move toward a bright future; she had youth on her side and the gift of time. I suggested this be our last meeting.

"One more week, please?" She reached across and took my hand.

"I can't imagine not having you to talk to every week, but give me time to get used to the idea." I smiled, enjoying the maternal role I was playing to this young mother, I gave in. "One more week," I said.

I rose from my chair, still holding her hand, "I'll see you next Thursday."

It would be two years before I saw Cassie again.

CHAPTER 2 – TOM

"It is better to have loved and lost, than never to have loved at all."
~Alfred Lord Tennyson

I wasn't supposed to be alone.

My good friend Patti insisted I go to the party, newly divorced and having been on my own with a two-year old for the past several months, I decided she may be right. It was November 1st, 1969, the height of the Vietnam war and the sexual revolution. Women were no longer confined to stereotypical roles of subservient housewives with pristine children tugging at their apron strings. We were enjoying a newfound freedom to explore relationships, rival males in the workplace and express ourselves as individuals with pride and purpose.

I was a purchasing agent for Beebe International, Inc., selling cranes, hoists and winches. It wasn't exactly glamorous, but it was a job that allowed me to take care of my son, Jeffery, and feel somewhat independent after a marriage that had been doomed for failure nearly from the beginning.

Alcohol flowed freely that night and it wasn't long before an obnoxious drunk, who was more than twice my size, pursued me. His advances were met with little enthusiasm, but his persistence was vigorous. Roger, the host of the party, suggested I escape to the local mini-mart with his friend Tom, who was headed out for cigarettes. I was so grateful for the opportunity to elude my inebriated pursuer, I didn't notice how handsome Tom was until we were several minutes into our journey for peace and nicotine.

The party ended with a request for my number and a hint that my life was about to change. I married Tom in a simple ceremony in the waterfront home he shared with four friends on April 18th, 1970. Tom moved into the tiny two-bedroom home I owned, until we eventually bought a three-bedroom split level in Kirkland, Washington.

Jeffery and Tom hit it off from the start; Tom slipped into the role of fatherhood with ease and Jeffery welcomed his strong male presence. It wasn't long before I began to feel that we were indeed a family and my sights shifted from a rickety past to a future with the man I was convinced was my soul-mate and the love of my life, and my young son.

I became pregnant and delivered a beautiful baby girl in January, 1972 and left my job to raise our family and tend to our household. I was happy in my role of caring for my children and wife to Tom. I never felt that I had put my own identity on hold; I found joy in giving to my family and the return on that investment was something I cherished. My only bout with grief in our happy home was the loss of our third child at birth, but I was determined to focus on the gifts life had given us, and not on what had been sadly taken away.

In 1977 Tom and I bought lakefront property and began the process of building our dream home. We moved in right around Thanksgiving in 1978 and for the next several years our life was bliss with friendly gatherings on our dock, teaching the kids watersports on the lake and making the compilation of wood, shingles and drywall, a home.

* * * *

Tina was the office skank. She flitted around flirting with all the married men, her remarks were often off-color and inappropriate and being a time before the threat of sexual harassment in the workplace, the men often engaged and encouraged the banter. The rumor mill was rife with tales of Tina's resolve toward seduction and Tom was not immune to her lascivious charms.

It wasn't long before I became suspicious, it was far more intuition than hard evidence, but I had a nagging feeling that the playful repartee had made its way from the office into the sheets—and I was right. The pain of deception was unlike anything I had felt before.

I couldn't get past the betrayal; I was furious at this horrible woman who had no regard for me or my family. I was beyond livid that she had selfishly sacrificed the security of my home with Tom, the sanctity of life as we knew it. I was furious at Tom for disregarding our marriage vows and ruining the beautiful life we had spent years building. No matter how I tried to see beyond the affair, no matter that Tina meant nothing more to Tom than a meaningless tumble in the hay, I was heartbroken and had a terrible desire to flee. We separated in November of 1987 and we divorced the following May. My life began to shift and for all intents and purposes—I was indeed—alone.

I was afraid—I hadn't been on my own since Jeffery was a baby and now he lived in a frat house at the University of Washington. He was a grown man and Michelle was just entering the mid-teen years, which were hard enough when the parents were together—throw a divorce into the mix and those years become even more tumultuous.

Tom kept his business and I was given the lake home. I took a job as a sales director as soon as our divorce was final and made a valiant attempt to embark on an existence of a single woman again. It wasn't easy, but I managed to keep the lake house for a few more years before selling it and relocating to Bellevue, Washington. I would be closer to a new job I had taken and I was beginning to feel that the lake house held too many memories, and while most of them were wonderful, they seemed to serve as a road block to my attempt to move on.

I leased a large home, but it felt painfully empty, I'd hear my footsteps echo in the halls. Gone were the sounds of family; the hustle and bustle of children preparing for school or the sounds of summer on the lake; the splash of swimmers, the thump of a speedboat's hull hitting the glimmering surface in the middle of July—the mouthwatering aroma of steaks on the grill; the simple clink of ice in a glass when the last drops of lemonade were savored by a stranger in a sandwich shop would send me reeling back to a simpler time and I ached to be there in the safe haven we had built.

Gone were the evenings where Tom and I shared the comings and goings of the day over a glass of coke or a cup of coffee—

sometimes hours would pass before we realized the sun had long set as we were immersed in intimate conversation. I missed our talks. I missed our marriage. I missed my life-love and I damned the demon who compromised my happiness in such a wicked way. I felt robbed and I needed to somehow take control of my life once more.

Michelle had moved in with friends after college and the new-found freedom allowed me to embark on new territory. It was me and only me that I needed to be truly concerned with, I left Bellevue and moved to Edmonds where I realized my long-time dream of owning my own business and purchased a drive-thru expresso shop and called it Caffé Aida. It was small, but it was mine and I was beginning to feel trickles of contentment in my new surroundings. I spent $52,000 to rebuild the shop and began dating Mike, the contractor. I named the café in honor of my mother and I was often chided by my Uncle John that it was my way of finally corralling my mother's love, I rarely argued that fact.

It was the winter of '92 when I leased my townhome. I put my personal touches everywhere and although it was only a rental, I made it my home. My experience as an advocate at the local rape crisis center taught me a great deal from doctors and detectives about both the medical and legal repercussions of a rape and my new-found expertise on the subject served to boost my confidence—with every individual I helped through the trauma of being violated, I felt myself emerge a little from the ashes of my failed marriage and found myself looking back at the pile of rubble less and less.

I wasn't supposed to be alone—but alone I was, and there was only one way to go—and that was forward.

Side note: Tom moved on, but never remarried. I'm grateful that I was able to forgive him before he passed away some years later. After his death, a close friend to both Tom and I would confide in me that Tom never stopped loving me; which was somewhat sad because I had never stopped loving him either. We were both too stubborn to admit it, but we were meant to be together to the end—I'm sorry that didn't happen.

Even with his one flaw, Tom was the love of my life.

CHAPTER 3 – COMING HOME

"In this hour, I do not believe that any darkness will endure."
~J.R.R. Tolkien

It was after 11:00pm when I pulled my Celica convertible onto my quiet suburban Edmonds street. It had been a beautiful, sunny mid-May day and while the sun had set hours earlier, it was still warm enough to have the top down; not always the case in the suburbs of Seattle.

It had been a long day, starting with my shift at Caffé Aida. The afternoon was a series of meetings with espresso bean and paper suppliers, followed by a much needed work-out at my local gym and topped off with a trip to the Seattle Coliseum to see the Supersonics take on the Houston Rockets along with 14,000 other die-hard fans; a game the Sonics would win 111-100.

I was beginning to feel at home in Edmonds. I found it to be a beautiful place; a quaint town with safe, upper-middle class neighborhoods where people shopped, dined and strolled their days away. I felt comfortable, and more importantly, I felt safe in the home I shared with Puka, my terrier-poodle mix.

The drive home from Seattle was an opportunity to unwind from the excitement of the game and having stopped at the coffee shop on my way home to check inventory for the following day and pick up the last shifts receipts, I had managed to return to the reality that made up my life.

I was tired and ready to fall into bed, but a few items of paperwork would take precedence. Late nights and very early mornings were the norm when it came to owning a coffee business, and I was no exception. I was well aware that 4:00am would roll around far too soon and dragging myself from the warmth of my comforter would be a chore, but when it came to seeing a great Sonics' game, well, some things were just worth it.

* * * *

I pulled to my row of townhomes and was a little taken aback to see what appeared to be a teen on Rollerblades. It seemed like an odd time of night to don a pair of skates and cruise a parking lot, but I wrote it off to the whimsy of youth and cautiously passed, pulled into my driveway and pressed my remote to raise my garage door. As I waited for the door to rise, I put up the convertible top and silently bid the lovely night air goodbye.

I pulled into the garage, shut off the engine and once again pressed the remote, closing the door behind me. Ever since my car alarm had been cut by a would-be thief while parked in my driveway some weeks earlier, I was extra cautious about staying inside the car until the door was all the way down. I glanced at my watch, it was 11:08pm and I took a deep breath, willing myself to re-energize for the hour or so of work still ahead of me.

I opened the trunk of the car and loaded it up with several sleeves of coffee cups and lids I'd need the following morning. I was fascinated by the power of the cups; once filled with a favorite beverage, they served to begin my clients' mornings with warmth and the promise of possibility the day held in store. I felt a little like the Caffeine fairy, loading them up with goodness and sending them off with light whip and a friendly smile. I was happy in that role.

I grabbed the bag of cash and receipts off the front seat and locked the car, the little beep helped me know my rag-top baby was indeed secure for the night and I stepped out onto the sidewalk that separated my unit from my neighbor's, pulled the door shut behind me and headed inside.

I turned my key and opened the door to my haven. Even in the dark of night my home appeared bright, cheerful and welcoming. White walls and appliances, off-white carpets, white mini-blinds; they all seemed to reflect even the slightest glimmer of light.

In the absence of children, what was white seemed to stay that way and I loved the simple elegance my décor offered. Tom and I had been through our share of hip-level fingerprints and crayon-marks on the walls, red juice and chocolate ice-cream stains in the carpet, and while I missed my family, I did enjoy coming home to a clean and tidy abode.

Puka met me with enthusiasm, even at fourteen she never hesitated to greet me with the excitement of a pup. Named after Michelle's favorite puka-shell bracelet that her grandparents had brought her from Hawaii when she was just five years old, Puka was my companion and it never came into question during the settlement who she would go with. It was clear she would always be mine.

I set down my purse and the bag of receipts and bent to give her a proper greeting. She had been alone for most of the day and while I knew deep down she enjoyed the hours of undisturbed slumber, I felt a little guilty.

"Want to go out?" I asked, as her tail wagged eagerly. I was grateful she had a strong bladder and, at least for now, my carpet remained free of little yellow hints of her imminent state of senior-hood. We'd cross that bridge when we came to it.

We stepped out front and into the small yard; Puka was engrossed in the smells that had collected throughout the day, but I was distracted with the sounds of skates on asphalt in the distance and then approaching. The young man from earlier zoomed by, shooting a glance our way before disappearing further down the parking lot. I didn't recognize him as a neighborhood local, but that didn't mean he wasn't someone's guest. I was a little annoyed that he broke the stillness of our quiet street so blatantly. Puka finished her business and we headed back inside, I could still hear the unwelcome visitor skate circles further down the parking lot as I closed and locked the door and secured the deadbolt.

I was exhausted and Puka never balked at the opportunity to curl up on her bed, so I took my purse and the receipts, turned off the kitchen light and we headed upstairs. I wanted to follow Puka into my room and fall into bed; instead I headed into the bedroom I used as an office and laid the moneybag on my desk.

My nightly ritual included preparing the bank deposit for the following day and this particular night included payroll for my employees. I decided to wash up and get into something cool before crunching the numbers. It had been an unseasonably warm day and the upper level was notorious for being ten degrees warmer than any other part of the house, so I was glad I had thought to open a few windows before leaving for the game.

I headed to my master bedroom. It was large enough to hold my queen four-poster bed, a pair of bed-side tables and two large chests of drawers—with room to spare. I quickly stripped down to my panties and slipped on my favorite crop-top I had purchased from the Hard Rock Café in Acapulco. It was sleeveless, cool and great for sleeping in.

It was off to the bathroom pull a brush through my long blonde hair and clip it high on my head before brushing and flossing my teeth and washing my face. It was tempting to ditch the paperwork in favor of my comforter, but I headed to the office. Puka didn't even follow me, the heat seemed to zap her energy as well.

As I counted the money I had an odd feeling, like I was being watched. I turned toward the closed blinds that led to the enclosed balcony and wrote my paranoia off to fatigue. I reached in my bottom desk drawer and into a box of plain white envelopes where I kept the key that opened the tall metal cabinet where I kept the cash. I opened the cabinet and took out the money and receipts from the morning shift and combined them with those I had brought that evening. I was pretty pleased with the totals, my café was doing better than I even anticipated and thoughts of opening a second location sometimes trickled into the back of my mind, but I knew in reality—for the moment anyway, I had my hands full.

Later, as I put the prepared deposit back in the cabinet and locked it, I once again had the strange feeling I was being watched, I moved to the balcony door and flipped on the light. I peered trough the mini-blinds and it was clear there was no one out there. I was tired and a little annoyed at myself for feeling like a seventh grade girl on her first after-dark babysitting stint, and decided it was definitely time for bed. I closed and locked the office window and shut out the light.

Back in my bedroom, I reached up to partially close the window. My landlord's alarm company had insisted that window need not be wired as no one could possibly ascend that high. I left it open some six inches and climbed into bed. I set my alarm for 4am and pressed my ear plugs into place. Having lived on Lake Tapps for fourteen years, I had grown accustomed to silent nights and the traffic from the nearby highway sometimes disrupted my ability to fall asleep, and so the little orange buds helped.

I turned off my bedside lamp, said my prayers and the last time I looked at the clock it read 12:04am; less than four hours before I was to get up and happily, albeit tiredly, greet the day. I drifted easily into a deep, inviting sleep.

Code 10-71 Victim to Victor A True Story

CHAPTER 4 – THE NIGHTMARE

"A nightmare has taken hold of my body. Lunacy has its way inside my mind."

~Amanda Steele

The dream was vivid—I was fighting a man and I was terrified. I could hear piercing screams and they seemed to be coming from me. I had been dragged from the bed to the floor and my head was repeatedly slammed into the sideboard of the bed and the floor.

I continued to scream, but I could hear his voice above the high-pitched wails; "Shut up!

We're going to kill you! Are you deaf? Can't you hear?! I said SHUT UP!" Something sharp stabbed into my left shoulder and the pain was excruciating. Oh dear God, this was really happening.

My body was drenched in sweat as I was held face down, his knee was trenched into my back. Again he slammed my head into the sideboard and shouted, "Shut up! We're going to kill you! Where are your guns?!"

I turned my head toward the booming voice, but his knee jammed even harder, "Don't look! Don't turn around! Keep your face down!" Who are they? How did they get in? How do they know I have guns? I was terrified, but somehow managed to get the words out, "In my purse."

I heard him continue to yell, but this time it wasn't at me, "No Charlie, don't leave! Stay! Don't go!" Then he was back on me with the sharp object piercing ever harder into my shoulder blade, "Where are your guns?! We're going to kill you!" It was clear he hadn't heard me and I second guessed helping them kill me.

My mind raced—Oh my God, they're going to kill me with my own guns! What about my children? I'll never see them again. I'll never get to enjoy grandchildren. Jeffery was engaged to a girl I had grown to love as my own daughter. I would not be here to see them marry. They lived just twenty minutes away and Michelle was an hour away working at a recreational supply company and served as a volunteer firefighter for the Lake Tapps fire department. I was so proud of them both, they were self- sufficient, making it on their own. They were strong and independent. They were my life.

I was sweltering and scared out of my mind as the sharp object continued to penetrate my flesh. Again he roared, "Tell us where your guns are! We're going to kill you! Shut up!" I stopped screaming, but I started to tremble and sob. My tears flowed and mixed with the drops of sweat, "I don't have any," I whimpered. He became even more bestial as he yelled into my ear, "We're going to rape you! Have you ever been raped?"

I was overcome with fear and any sense of hope that I could escape the unthinkable was quickly vanishing, "No. Please no. Those are my kids pictures on the wall. I'm too old."

"We don't care how old you are! Don't turn around or we'll kill you right now!"

I needed time, maybe they wouldn't kill me if I just did what they said. I never did hear Charlie speak—Did he leave? Is he watching? I began to feel numb as he took his knee from my back and ripped my shirt off in what seemed like a split second. He slammed my head to the floor and exclaimed, "I'm going to feel your breasts!" A wave of nausea came over me as he reached around and placed his hand on my left breast. On impulse I jerked back and cried out, he slammed my head into the sideboard, "I won't kill you if you be quiet!"

I was now totally numb, I was aware of what was happening, but seemed to have detached and felt as though I were watching a horror movie unfold. *This could not happen in my world!*

"We're gonna get up on the bed. But don't turn around or we'll kill you right now!" His breathing grew heavier as he seemed to be getting worked up. I wanted to live, even though I had to endure this horror. *Maybe, just maybe they'll find some bit of compassion and let me live when they're done with me.*

They had total control now, I was their slave and I was to follow orders. I had little feeling as I struggled to get up and lay face down on the bed. There was blood—a lot of blood—that seemed to be coming from me, even though I felt nothing. He quickly became irritated, "Where are you bleeding from?" he yelled. "I don't know," I cried. He smashed my face to the sheets.

He ordered me to place my hands behind me and I felt him wrap something soft around my left hand, "You're not hurt that bad," he said. "I won't kill you if you do this right." I began to think about my children and the tears flowed.

"I'm gonna blindfold you now, you try and look at me and I'll kill you right now!" His excitement peaked as he knew he was in complete control. He was the triumphant one as he covered my eyes with a cloth and tied it tight behind my head. It covered a portion of my nose and made it difficult to breathe, instinctively I pushed it up with my hands and he went ballistic, "If you look at me or try to take it off—I swear I'll kill you!"

"I can't breathe," I said. He didn't care, he was barbaric, enraged—like a mad dog. He ordered me to turn over and terror-stricken, I did. He yanked off my panties and then all was deadly quiet—Is he taking off his clothes?

I heard the click of the crystal lamp next to the bed and imagined the room was now flooded with light, but could see none as the blindfold was soaked with tears. "Spread your legs!" he commanded. I was mortified as I complied—*He's a beast! He's going to stick his knife in me! Please God, don't let him torture me. Let me die quickly, with no more pain!* Instead, I felt his fingers penetrate me.

"Do you have any lubricant?" His voice sounded aroused. "No," I cried. My sobs were loud and out of control and he was furious. He shoved his penis in my vagina and snapped, "Just lay there—don't move!" His breathing quickened as he thrust back and forth for the next ten minutes. He suddenly pulled out, grabbed me and screeched, "Now, get up!"

He pulled me off the bed and pressed the sharp object into my shoulder once again. The pain made me move, I was his personal robot. *My dog! Where is my dog? Surely she would have barked or attacked him! He killed my dog! He must have killed my dog!*

He shoved me to the foot of the bed, "Get on your knees! You're gonna do this and if you bite me, I'll slit your throat!" He put what I now knew was a knife to my throat and pressed hard as my mind raced—Get it over with, just kill me! Don't put me through this humiliation!

He demanded I open my mouth and put his penis in as he continued to hold the knife firmly to my throat. "Lick it!" he snapped. I licked it, but was so violently repulsed that my mouth was completely parched. He pulled me to my feet and forced me back on the bed, this time face up. He climbed on and pushed my legs apart. I felt his tongue penetrate me as he began performing oral sex. I was stunned, I had never heard of a rapist doing this to a victim, but then I had never been a victim.

I thought I knew everything there was to know about rape. Having been trained by both doctors and detectives, I had helped numerous victims, both male and female, to navigate the aftermath of attacks, from the emergency rooms, to depositions and often the entire court process. What I was realizing during my own horror was that I really knew very little about what it was to be violated in such a grossly inhumane way.

He continued to lick and suck as his tongue made its way up my stomach and to my breasts where he lapped at one, and then the other. I felt facial hair—a mustache, and realized I must remember that detail if he let me live. He grabbed my face and began kissing my mouth. He tried to force his tongue through my clenched lips—I wasn't going to aid this animal in his reign of terror.

"Put your legs up!" he demanded, I could tell my lack of response was aggravating him. I raised my legs and he thrust himself inside me once more, he draped one leg over his shoulder and forced the other to the bed. His breathing quickened as he continued to rape me. The thrusts slowed as his breathing eased and he took my leg from his shoulder and placed it back on the bed, then began kissing my breasts and mouth once more.

"Tell me you like it!" he ordered, "Act like you like it!" When he began raping me he told me to, "Just lay there! Don't move!" Now he wanted me to behave as his lover. He could go to hell as far as I was concerned. I wasn't going to play that game.

"Put your arms around me!" he snarled. I placed my hands to the sides of his waist and noted there was no fat. He was lean and I concluded he was young. "Tell me you like this!" he repeated. I didn't utter a sound. My blindfold was drenched and I wondered when my body would be drained of all fluid.

"I have a little dick, don't I, lady?" I shook my head, indicating "no", to have told him the truth might have transformed him from rapist to murderer and I couldn't take that chance. "You can tell the truth. You can tell me I have a little dick, I won't kill you for that." I refused to respond and he pulled out and went back to kissing my clenched lips. I must have done the right thing by lying to him.

He straddled me and entered once more, this time he sat upright. His thrusts became faster and more urgent, I thought he was never going to stop. He pulled out and said, "I'm gonna come and I'm gonna come in your mouth! So, get ready!" He shimmied up to my chest and I could barely breathe, I could hear him using his hand to keep his erection as he mounted my ribcage.

I was willing to die at this point rather than comply, I refused to lay a hand on him as he yelled, "Open your mouth!" I gritted my teeth and kept my lips tightly sealed as he ejaculated onto my chest, neck, chin and clenched mouth. I would give up nothing more, I'd rather die than suffer any further indignity. I was certain he would kill me for disobeying, instead he took his hand and caressed my breasts with his semen. I was repulsed and couldn't move.

"Just lay there," he ordered. I could hear him put his clothes back on, then he grabbed me and jerked me off the bed. I was unsteady on my feet and my equilibrium was off.

"You're gonna show me where the money is!" He stated. I feigned ignorance, "What money?" He became angry and snapped, "I've been watching you and I know you keep it in that metal thing."

This monster had just robbed me of my last ounce of dignity and now he wanted my money? I silently vowed that enough was enough and I would not cooperate with yet another violation.

"What metal thing?" I asked. He was getting impatient and while I knew I was dealing with a dangerous beast, something inside of me begged to be empowered and not give in to this maniac any more than I already had.

"The tall one with the two doors," he snarled. He was poking my back with the knife again. "Now where's the key?" I wondered how he knew I had the money locked up. He must have somehow watched me, but how? I had always closed the blinds to my second floor office before counting the day's receipts and preparing the deposit.

"Is the key upstairs or downstairs?" he demanded. "It's upstairs," I relented.

"Where did you get the money?" he asked.

I knew I couldn't tell him, because if I somehow lived through this horror, I knew he'd be back for more. I was well aware I'd never survive anything like this again.

"It's not mine," I insisted, "it belongs to a guy I know, he can't keep it at his place." His lack of response told me he believed me, as he marched me down the hall to my office. It was a room with a closet, a bathroom, a window and a glass door that led to an enclosed balcony.

There were no stairs leading to the balcony. *How could he have gotten up here?*

CHAPTER 5 – TURNING THE TABLES

"I will not die without fighting for a life I am not done living."
~Bethany Wiggins

The nightmare continued as he dragged me into my office and demanded I tell him where I kept the key to the cabinet. The knife pierced my back as he yelled, "Where's the key? Tell me where the key is!"

His agitation continued to increase as he prodded me with the knife. I realized my life was far more precious than the contents of the cabinet and told him what he wanted to know, "In the bottom drawer," I said.

He held the knife with his right hand and reached for the drawer with his left, so while he had a hold on the knife, he no longer had a hold on me. My head filled with frantic thoughts of fleeing; *This is my chance! I can run down the stairs and out the front door. Can I make it? Can I outrun him? Will he kill me if he catches me? I'll scream! Surely someone will hear me and call the police. If I don't run, he'll kill me once he has the key. Where is Charlie? I never heard him speak, is he still here?*

The sharp pain of the knife and the horrid voice brought me back to the here and now. I could hear him rummaging through the bottom drawer, "Is it in the brown bag?" he demanded.

I tried to buy time, "Yes," I said. I willed my feet to move, but to no avail. I was paralyzed in place. *Run! I've got to try!*

"It's not there!" he screamed, "Where is it?"

"It's in the box of envelopes!" I could hear him rummage further and one thought screamed in my brain, *Now! Run!*

I yanked at the blindfold, but didn't look at the monster, I was on a mission. I was convinced I could hit the top of the stairs in three swift strides, then I'd run down the stairs, through the living room and down the hall to the front door. The door was locked with a dead bolt as well as a regular lock, I would have to be fast. A childhood memory of my ability to run the bases in baseball like a little gazelle flashed before me and I was suddenly fearless.

I was in my second stride toward the stairs when he tackled me from behind, slamming me to the carpet, my body hit the floor like a sledgehammer. The breath was knocked out of me as he came down hard on my back and straddled me. He grabbed my head and jerked it back as he bellowed, "Now I'm gonna kill you! I'm gonna break your neck and slit your throat!"

He was rabid and frenzied as he twisted my head hard to the right, again and again he tried to snap my neck. His right hand slid across my face and two fingers slipped into my mouth.

A rush of adrenaline surged through my body as I bit down hard on his fingers. I clenched my jaw tight as he screeched in pain. He punched my head with his left fist and I reached back and grabbed his genitals. I twisted and squeezed with all my might, and held him in a vise grip. I clamped down hard and no amount of punches were going to get me to release him. *I had him now!*

The beast morphed into a pathetic beggar, "Let go! Let go and I'll leave." I didn't believe him. I had the control now and I wasn't about to relinquish it; I almost enjoyed inflicting the pain and suffering on him. I felt electrified as the adrenaline pumped through my veins. I was suddenly the powerful one; woman of steel— invincible.

He cried out in excruciating pain, "Let go! Let go and I'll leave!" I didn't recognize my voice, it sounded monstrous as I made my own demands through clenched teeth, "No! Stand up!" I knew I couldn't trust him to leave and I only wanted to get him to the front door and throw him out. I just wanted the nightmare to be over.

He was the helpless one now, my plan was to get him out of my house, then I'd call the police and my children. He moved to get to his feet and my grasp to his genitals tightened—I was still in control. As I pulled myself up, he somehow managed to rip his fingers from my mouth. I grabbed for his hair and it came off in my hands—*A wig?*

I dropped the wig and he took advantage of the split second and his foot came crashing into my chest with such force that I was once again flat on my back. I gasped for breath as his foot came down again and again, he was vicious—relentless.

My arms and legs flailed as I tried desperately to block his foot. He was crazed as he stomped on me again and again; my chest, my face, my head—I tried to fight back, but he was so strong I could not breathe, let alone get off my back. The blows to my body were fierce and fatigue was overtaking me. Is this what it is to be bludgeoned to death?

I silently bid my precious children goodbye. I was suffocating from the blows, my arms and legs fell still. *Play dead!*

The pain was too great to bear and I felt myself slipping away. I lay perfectly still as he continued to stomp on me—and finally stopped. He was gasping for air as he knelt to make sure I was no longer a threat to him. Does he think I've passed out? Does he think I'm dead?

I desperately hung on to consciousness as he turned me on my side. I could barely make out the closets that lined the hallway, Charlie must have gone. Maybe there never was a Charlie.

He left me incapacitated and made his way back to my office. I heard him ransack my office in search of the key to the cabinet that held the bank deposit.

I lay still and whimpered in pain, he heard me gasp for air and shouted, "Shut up or I'll kill you right now!" I was dazed and confused and without thought I said, "I have to go to the bathroom, please let me go to the bathroom." He yelled back at me, "No! You can go after!"

"Please, I have to go." I didn't have to go, but I was desperate for an escape from him. Any sanctuary would do and the bathroom with a door to stand between him and I was the best I had for the moment. I inched my way in the direction of my bedroom, each movement became a painful reminder of what I had just endured.

Suddenly he grabbed me and pulled me to my feet, he was visibly annoyed and I braced myself for another beating that never came. Instead he shoved me into my bedroom and then toward the master bath, "Get in there! Lock the door and stay there!"

"The door doesn't lock," I said and instantly regretted it. I owed this maniac no explanations and thankfully it didn't seem to register that he still had easy access to me behind an unlocked door. "Just stay in there!" he demanded, and slammed the door. I was alone in the bathroom, thoughts flooded my aching head, *I need a weapon! I need something to use against him when he returns to finish me off.*

I opened the cabinet and grabbed a toenail scissors. It was the best defense available to me at that moment. *Is he outside the door? Will he barge in at any minute?*

I reached into the cabinet and pulled out the rubbing alcohol. Perhaps if he heard me urinating he wouldn't enter. I poured the alcohol into the toilet—the stream of liquid would serve to buy me time. I placed the alcohol beside the toilet and flushed. My eyes darted to my inferior weapon, I don't stand a chance against him and his knife, I thought.

With the blindfold off, he knew I might identify him and that was too risky. It was clear he would have to kill me. I'd been in an adrenaline-enraged blind state when I fought him and I had no recollection of what he looked like, only he didn't know this.

The toilet tank was refilling when I remembered my gun. I had left it in an attaché purse on a dresser outside the bathroom door. I didn't know where he was and couldn't hear a thing above the flowing tank water. *It's him or me! I surmised, kill or be killed.*

I slowly opened the door—I could hear him still rummaging in my office, the purse was where I had left it and I slowly reached for it, drew it into the bathroom and quietly closed the door. I reached into the purse; wallet, checkbook, hand lotion, photos of my children—everything was there but the gun. I began to shake as I dug deeper, Please God, help me find my gun! I had never used it on anyone and considered myself an average shot, but now I was prepared to slaughter—*I will kill him before he kills me!*

I was nearly frantic when my hand felt the cool hard metal in the bottom of my purse, a wave of relief washed over me as I pulled it out. The magazine was in and loaded, but I would have to engage it by pulling back the slide lock. My left hand was bleeding badly and it hurt to attempt to engage a bullet. I only needed to secure one bullet into the firing position and the semi-automatic would fire multiple times.

There lied the problem, in the past I had had multiple difficulties getting the bullet to properly engage. It would end up in an angled position locking the slide-lock open and rendering the gun useless. When it had happened before I was never able to disengage the bullet on my own, I simply wasn't strong enough, a male counterpart would have to help me. I once even asked a policeman to aid me in disengaging the angled bullet.

My hand hurt terribly and the blood made it impossible to get a decent hold on the weapon. I grabbed a bath towel and wrapped the grip panel. I was sweating profusely as I struggled with the slide lock. "God help me," I whispered. Ignoring the pain in my hand I pulled back the slide mechanism and released it. Just like always, a bullet sprang up at an angle and the slide locked in the open position—the gun was useless.

I was filled with panic, my heart was pounding in my throat as I pulled the slide lock again, this time using the towel to give me a tighter grip. It worked! A bullet properly engaged in the firing position and the gun was ready to shoot.

I slowly opened the door, terrified I stepped out of the bathroom. I held the gun down by my side. I was terrified when I saw him enter the bedroom, the knife held in a position to stab just four feet from me. Without hesitating I brought my gun up, my arms fully extended and both hands on the grip. I was shaking so bad; I was convinced I'd never be able to hit my target.

His eyes went wide when he saw the gun, "No! No!" he yelled in a horrific tone. He sprung from the room and I vaulted after him. He was down the hall at the top of the steps, about to leap down the stairs when the first shot rang out. It hit the wall; I barely missed him. He was halfway to the landing when I threw myself over a half wall of the staircase and fired again—then a third time—and a fourth—and a fifth. I pulled the trigger one last time and heard the click of an empty gun as he vanished out of sight. My heart was pounding as if it were about to burst.

Did he hear the click of an empty gun? Did I hit him? He will surely kill me now. He didn't come back and I couldn't hear him. I feared he was wounded or dead on my living room floor. I slowly descended the stairs, my gun at my side, even though it was empty, I still had a grip of death on it.

He was at the front door, trying frantically to open it, but couldn't seem to figure out the lock. "Don't kill me! Don't kill me!" It was then that I understood he didn't know my gun was empty. I held it up, point blank at my attacker. He ran into the powder room, which was small with no window. He had nowhere to go, he would have to face me.

The tables were turned, the monster who raped me—beat me—tried to kill me, was at my mercy, I now had total control. Whether my gun was loaded or not, he believed it was and he knew I was capable of pulling the trigger. I suddenly felt unconquerable.

I stood in the kitchen, facing the open door to the powder room and yelled, "I'm gonna kill you, you mother fucker!" He pleaded in return, "No, no. Please just let me go." His back was pressed to the wall, the knife in one hand and the money bag in the other.

"Throw that bag out here!" I demanded, he complied, throwing it at me hard. It hit me and fell to the floor, not taking my eyes off him I reached for it and threw it in the dishwasher. As I slammed the dishwasher door, he lurched for the open door, but was frozen by my orders—"I'll kill you! You mother fucker! Get on your fucking knees! Now!"

He instantly dropped to his knees, still facing me. "You move again and I'll blow your head off!" I roared, "Put your hands behind your head!"

"Please don't kill me," he begged.

I demanded that he lay face down on the floor, and as he eased himself down I realized I was now the monster and he was pleading for his life. This desire to kill was something I'd never experienced before, If only I had more bullets! *God, I wish I had more bullets!*

The powder room was small and he had to draw his knees to his chest to meet my demands. He continued to whimper and beg for mercy, but he never apologized for what he had done to me and that made me furious. He was a narcissistic bastard who would surely rape again, in fact I was certain that next time he would kill his victim to ensure he'd never be in a position of entrapment again.

I knew the patterns from my training with Pierce County Rape Relief. He had likely done this before and he would surely do it again. The infamous Ted Bundy had started with pornography, then became a peeping-tom. When such activities fail to excite them any longer, they turn to rape and when that's no longer enough, they turn to murder. Rape is nothing more than an exercise of power over another, having nothing to do with attraction. We had victims range from two months to ninety-two years old.

I continued to hold the gun on him as I reached for the speaker phone with my bloody left hand and pressed 911. It felt like minutes had passed and nothing happened, I panicked, I must have pushed the wrong buttons!

He was obviously uncomfortable curled up on the floor and began to move, "Don't you move or I'll blow your head off!" I threatened. He became still and I grabbed the phone from its cradle. I held the gun firm, I didn't want him to think I would ease up in any way, I once again pushed 911 and this time it rang.

A female voice answered:

Operator: Nine-one-one, what are you reporting?

Me: Get over here! *Run!* I've been raped and I've got a gun! *I'll kill him!*

Operator: Ma'am!

Me: *I'll kill him!*

Operator: Ma'am!

Me: My address is 7730 196th Street, South-West

Operator: Stop screaming!

Me: Unit number nine.

Operator: Ma'am!

Me: What?

Operator: Stop screaming because I cannot hear you! Calm down!

Me: Seven-seven-three-zero.

Operator: Yes.

Me: One-hundred-ninety-sixth street south-west, Edmonds.

Operator: House or apartment?

Me: Unit nine!

Operator: What's the name of the complex?

Me: Wind and Wood! I'll kill him! I shot him!

Operator: Ma'am! Ma'am! Ma'am!

Me: What?

Operator: When did this happen?

Me: He's still here! Hurry up!

Operator: Okay, stay on the line. I'll get the officers started.

Me: Hurry up!

Operator: Are you injured?

Me: Yes!

Operator: Do you know who he is?

Me: No!

Operator: He's still in your apartment?

Me: Yes! I've got a gun on him right now and I'll blow his head off!

Operator: Stay o the line! Stay on the line!

Me: Okay! Hurry up!

Operator: Stay on the line!

Me: I will kill you!

Operator: Are you in Lynnwood or Edmonds?

Me: Edmonds. Sir! I'll kill you if you move! I will wrap nothing! I will blow your fucking head off! I will kill you and I have people that'll kill you if I don't! Don't move! Don't you move!

Operator: Okay ma'am, stay on the line.

Me: Hurry up!

Operator: You're doing fine, stay calm!

Me: Hurry up!

Operator: I have officers on the way.

Me: Hurry! I...I—how soon?

Operator: Okay, listen. They are on the way. Now, just listen to me and stay on the phone with me.

Me: Send an aid car too, please, and I want you to call someone else for me.

Operator: Okay, just wait a second.

Me: (to rapist) No! You move your hand again and I'll...I'll...

Officer's voice (filtered in background): I'm going that way.

Operator: Okay ma'am, you're doing really good. Stay as calm as you can.

Me: (to rapist) I will kill you! I will kill you!

Operator: Okay, okay, I understand that.

Me: I want to kill him!

Operator: Okay, okay, ma'am are you...ma'am?

Me: What?!

Operator: Did he use a weapon or anything?

Me: Yes!

Operator: Okay, what kind of injuries do you have?

Me: Um...it's my hand or something.

Operator: I want you to stay on the line. You're doing a good job.

Me: (to rapist) Are you staying calm yet?

Operator: Ma'am, ma'am!

Me: I hope not...I want to do it so bad!

Operator: Ma'am, ma'am! Stay as calm as you can and listen to me.

Me: Yes?

Operator: What race is he?

Me: White.

Operator: About how old is he?

Me: (to rapist) How old are you? How old are you going to be when you die?!

(then) Twenty-one he says.

Operator: Okay, okay. Are you bleeding?

Me: What?

Operator: Are you bleeding from the hand?

Me: Yes, I am!

Operator: Okay, stay on the line and I'll get an aid car going.

Me: I want you to call someone for me right away!

Operator: Okay.

Me: (to rapist) You move and I'll kill you, you son-of-a-bitch!

The phone hits the floor as there is pounding on the door. My gun discharges its last bullet, which hits the metal door and ricochets into the wall at the end of the entry hall.

Officer: Where is he?! Put your gun down!

Voice on tape: Shots fired.

Me: Ma'am, please call...

Operator: Ma'am, who is in there with you?

Me: The officers.

With that I handed the phone to the officer who identified himself, all the while keeping his gun poised on my attacker. I later learned that what seemed like hours for officers to arrive after initiating the call to 911, was a mere fifty-three seconds.

My understanding of time would never be the same again.

CHAPTER 6 – HELP ARRIVES

"Blessed are the Police Officers, for they protect our lives, guard our safety and keep the peace."

~Unknown

The pounding to my door was fierce, "Police! Open up!" My already heightened state was further hyped as I wondered how I'd navigate my path to the door, which would take me a mere two feet from the man I had tricked into thinking I still held a loaded gun to him. I was terrified he'd lunge for me before I could get to the door and let the officers in. Again I heard, "Police! Open up!"

My attacker lay face down on the powder room floor, his hand clutched his head, I saw this as my opportunity to make it to the door. I kept the gun pointed toward the powder room as I turned the deadbolt with my left hand and then unlocked the door. I tried to turn the knob but my hand was slick with blood and I couldn't get a grip, the knife wound to my left hand dripped incessantly preventing me from opening the door.

I looked toward the powder room and I was no longer in his field of vision, I grabbed the door knob with both hands and turned just as a bullet exploded from the chamber of the gun. I was stunned and instantly furious; there had been a bullet lodged in there this whole time I believed I was holding an empty gun. Had I known there was a bullet left, I would have meticulously aimed it for the worthless, sick monster's head and ended the nightmare for good.

I had never experienced such an intense desire to kill before. It was overwhelming.

I opened the door to the officer who held his gun with both arms extended, ready to shoot if necessary. "Where is he?" he demanded. "He's in the powder room," I responded and waved my gun in that direction. He moved toward the powder room and fixed his gun on the suspect, then quickly glanced back at me and in a reassuring tone instructed me to put my gun down. I bent down and laid my gun on the foyer floor.

The next few moments were a blur of police officers, entering my home and searching for any additional intruders. As each one entered, they'd glance at me and without a word, quickly look away. I was dazed and confused and wondered why they wouldn't look at me or speak to me, then I looked down and realized I was naked.

I was mortified and quickly moved to a corner of the kitchen where I cowered and tried desperately to cover myself with my hands and arms. I began to sob as the reality of what was happening began to come into focus. Officer L.P. Miller, a handsome man whom I vaguely recognized but couldn't place, grabbed a blanket from my living room couch and brought it to where I was huddled in the kitchen. He carefully wrapped it around me and led me to the living room and helped lower me onto the love seat.

"Do you remember me?" He asked. His delivery was kind and gentle, but he was met with a blank stare from me. It was clear my current state would not allow me to think clearly.

"I took the report when someone tried to steal your car," he offered.

Of course! I remembered now, it had been nearly three months earlier when I got in my car, destined for work at 4:30am, only to find it wouldn't start. A call to AAA would bring a tow truck to my door. With a check under the hood, the driver determined that the wires to my car alarm had been cut, along with a few other wires.

"Someone tried to steal your car," he said. "You'd be wise to file a police report." I had let Puka out at 3:30am and must have scared the thief off.

Later that day I contacted the police and they sent Officer Miller to file the report. He was thorough and professional and suggested I might want to keep my car in the garage from then on, as the make and model of my car was a favorite among car thieves.

As I sat there, it suddenly occurred to me that I was being victimized; the car and now the intrusion. I shivered at the thought that I was somehow—unbeknownst to me, under a scope for predators. They had tried to take my car and now succeeded in robbing me of my dignity and sense of safety. *What next? Would they be back for more?*

I shuddered at the thought, I was snapped out of my daze by another officer named Guthrie, "Where did you shoot him?" he asked. I didn't know I had!

Sobs prevented me from answering, one of the officers gently lifted something from around my neck and pulled it over my head. It was a lavender bandanna—the blindfold that had been brought into my home and used to render me sightless to my attacker.

Someone asked me if I wanted them to call my pastor. I stared blankly and they asked again, "Is there a minister or pastor we can call?" I wondered if they knew something I didn't, "I'm not going to die, am I?" They didn't mention it again.

The memory is vague, but somehow they laid me on a gurney. I was still wrapped in the blanket that Officer Miller had placed around me. I didn't know where the animal that had brutalized me was, but I knew the police had him.

As they took me out the front door, I was met by my neighbor, Lauren. Tears streamed down her face as she took my hand in hers. I looked down to see the deep cut between my thumb and forefinger. It was odd that I felt no pain, I was numb and had no idea how badly I was hurt.

"Oh, my God! Look what he did to her!" While her words were alarming, Lauren's familiar face was a welcome sight amongst the chaos and flurry of unfamiliar officers. We had always been friendly as we came and went about our days. Lauren lived alone as well and she and I had often promised to make a point of sharing a meal, but never got around to it. I suddenly felt a bond with her I'd not felt before, her tears told me she cared and I was comforted by that thought.

I don't recall being transported to Stevens Memorial Hospital in Edmonds, but I do remember Sergeant Debbie Smith, she stayed with me for quite a while in the hospital. She was kind and comforting as she took the necessary photos for the police files.

The emergency room nurse asked if there was anyone I would like them to call and Jeffery and Michelle immediately came to mind. She dialed Jeffery's number and handed me the phone. It was 3:00am and I couldn't imagine how awful it was for one to be jarred out of a sound sleep with your mother's words of, "I've been raped."

He told me he'd leave right away and I asked that he call Michelle before he got on the road and he said he would. I gave the nurse Mike's telephone number. He and I had stopped seeing one another a few months earlier, but we remained good friends and that's what I needed right now. Mike was a few minutes from the hospital, Jeffery was twenty minutes away and Michelle was a good hour from Edmonds.

Mike told the nurse he was on his way. My final call was to an employee of the coffee shop. I explained that I needed her to open the shop at 5:00am and she assured me she would. It was one less thing to worry about, she was a good employee and I needed her now more than ever.

Mike arrived and the look on his face told me that he was appalled at what had happened. Having been a volunteer firefighter years before, he had seen his share of the wounded, but he took my hand and assured me that I'd be okay and I instinctively knew I would be.

Next to arrive was Michelle. She had been too upset to drive, so her roommate, Stephanie had driven. I would later learn that Jeffery woke her out of a deep sleep at 3:00am with the words, "Michelle, first I want you to know that no one is dead." He then told her about the rape and where I was. She and Stephanie jumped in the car and sped to Edmonds. I felt lucky that they hadn't been killed getting to me. They arrived before Jeffery and his fiancé Lily made it to the hospital.

CHAPTER 7 – A FAMILY UNITED IN MAYHEM

"When everything goes to hell, the people who stand by you without flinching – they are your family."

~Jim Butcher

The phone roused Michelle out of a sound sleep, she glanced at the clock and immediately knew that something was wrong. For most people, the ring of the phone at 3a.m. was rarely a bearer of good news, or a friend in search of pre-dawn conversation.

She braced herself as she said, "Hello," and it was Jeffery's voice on the other end. He assured her that no one was dead, but that she needed to get to Edmonds, "Mom's been raped."

The words hung in mid-air as she tried to process what was being said. Her darkened room only served to add to the confusion as she teetered on the threshold between dream and reality, *Is this a nightmare? Wake up, Michelle! Wake up!*

It was no dream.

* * * *

The doors to the emergency room flew open and Michelle came running in. She stopped short at the sight of several police officers standing around sipping coffee, "What the hell is going on?!" She demanded. One officer spun on his heel and was equally abrupt, "Wait a second! Who are you?"

Michelle was livid, "You're standing around drinking coffee? Really?! Shouldn't you be looking for a rapist? You'd better hope I don't find him first! Where is my mom?"

The officers were pretty certain they knew who she was by this time, "Calm down! We've got the guy!" Once she was able to steady herself, they let her in to see me. She instantly broke down and sobbed, but quickly composed herself as she put her training as a volunteer firefighter to work and took control. There was a palpable role reversal as she became the parent and me, the child. I was the one in need of comforting and she held my hand as she interrogated the emergency room doctor and nurses as to what each test was for as they poked, prodded and tended to my wounds.

Jeffery and Lily arrived shortly after Michelle and Stephanie. They came into my room and put on brave faces as they told me they were there for me. I felt relief from Jeffery as I gave him instructions on what needed to be done for the coffee shop; while I had managed to get someone to open, she would need the till money by 5:15am. He felt helpless in fixing what had happened to his mother—at least he could put some of the pent-up energy toward the shop. He assured me it would all be taken care of.

Jeffery and Lily left the room while the ER staff administered the necessary tests conducted on a rape victim. They gathered hair and semen samples to be sent off to the lab for DNA testing. The results would be used to prosecute the suspect.

I knew exactly what they needed to do, my years as a rape relief counselor had me at many-a-bedside comforting victims as they were put through one humiliating, albeit necessary, test after another. The difference was that I was the victim this time.

They pulled twelve hairs, roots intact, from various parts of my scalp. They combed my pubic area in search of possible strays from my attacker and they performed a vaginal exam for possible trauma and semen samples. When I told them he had ejaculated on my chest, chin and closed lips, they gathered samples from my chest and swabbed my mouth with a large Q-tip. They took blood samples and tested for venereal disease. It was terrifying to think I could be given a disease.

They suggested I get tested for HIV in three months, explaining that the body takes up to three months to show cell changes once the virus has been contracted. I was confused and overwhelmed, I wasn't certain I could get through the next twelve hours and here I was being instructed on what to do three months from the worst moment of my life.

They asked when was the last time I had intercourse and I had no trouble remembering the last time I had been intimate with

Mike, "The first week in February," I managed. It was odd thinking back on the mutually loving and trusting act of making love and then being catapulted back to the here and now of the vile, violent act of rape.

They took chest x-rays and x-rays of my face. I was beginning to have some feeling back and I was in pain. There was concern that my heart was bleeding, and if so, they'd have to admit me to the hospital, an EKG would reveal that although my heart and the lining around it were badly bruised, it was not bleeding. I was relieved because all I wanted was to get out of there and get back to my life.

An officer poked his head in and said I'd need to stop by the Lynnwood Police Station sometime in the next several days to give a recorded statement.

"Well, it'll have to be in the next couple of hours. I have a business to run," I snapped. Little did I know I would not engage in the day to day operation of Caffé Aida for the next six weeks.

With my laundry list of injuries, I felt lucky to be alive. In addition to my bruised and swollen heart and tender sternum, I had a fractured nose, a swollen lip, six lacerations to my left shoulder, lesions on my right shoulder and left elbow consistent with friction burns, a cut to my upper left arm, the deep wound to my left hand, contusions on my thighs, lower legs and back, and my baby toe on my left foot was broken, along with two broken teeth from biting his fingers to the bone. It was difficult to breathe and the littlest movement caused me great pain. I was given a large dose of antibiotics and instructed to visit a ear, nose and throat doctor when the swelling to my nose subsided.

It was a little after eight when they told me I could leave the hospital, both Michelle and Jeffery told me I could stay with them, but I opted to stay with Mike, he was local and right here where I could get back to the business I loved.

They allowed me to shower and gave me surgical scrubs to wear as I had been brought in naked, with only a blanket to cover me. I let the hot water run over me for a long time, as if it could somehow sterilize me from the disgusting encounter with the animal. I had a strong desire to take a knife and scrape away my skin and the filth that had been embedded in me. I'm not certain how long I stood under the stream of warmth, but I finally came to terms that the one thing it could not wash away was the memory.

Michelle helped me dress and led me to Stephanie's car. Jeffery and Lily drove ahead of us and led the way to the Lynnwood Police Station where I would give my sworn statement. It was excruciating to try and extract myself from Stephanie's car, Jeffery and Michelle flanked me and helped me into the station.

Many officers looked my way with sympathetic stares as we entered, they seemed to know who I was. I felt awkward and a little humiliated as I wondered if any of them had seen me naked the night before.

There had been some whispers back in the ER about my attacker possibly being the serial rapist that had been on a recent rampage of attacking local women. While none had been killed, as of yet—they speculated that it was only a matter of time. I didn't think much about it and only regretted that I wasn't aware of the final bullet in the chamber. I could have saved everyone a lot of time and trouble.

Detective Jeff Jones from the Edmonds Police Department and Detective Joe Bruce from the Lynnwood Police Department gently explained that we would go to a private room where I would make my statement. Jeffery, Michelle, Lily and Stephanie were advised to wait in chairs while my statement was tape-recorded.

Michelle would have nothing to do with it, she took hold of my arm and stood by my side. "Miss, you'll have to wait," said Detective Bruce, "she'll be fine." Michelle held her ground, "She wants me with her."

The two detectives exchanged glances and relented, "You'll have to remain perfectly quiet, even if your mother becomes upset."

"I get it," said my loyal and stoic daughter.

They led us into a small room and were kind as they settled me into a chair, Detective Jones let me know that he had been at my home the night before. I didn't recognize him, but wrote that off to the flurry of uniforms that filed in and out of my front door during the ordeal. I only remembered the first responders, Officer L.P. Miller and Sergeant Debbie Smith, both from the Edmonds Police Department.

Detective Bruce sat beside me and controlled the tape recorder as I recounted my memory of the horror that took place only hours before. I chronologically told of each detail; including that of a possible second suspect that I never heard speak.

The detective asked me if I owned a gray stocking cap, which I did not. I wondered if that was the thing I had pulled from his head during my fight to stay alive.

When I got to the part where I had the suspect face down in the powder room, I was suddenly embarrassed to continue, "I was terrified," I confessed, "I wanted him to think I still had a loaded gun, I was yelling and swearing. Do I have to tell you what I said?" I considered Michelle, within earshot, hearing her mother rattle off expletives like some rap king.

"Go ahead," said Detective Bruce, "everyone understands that these were the most stressful moments of your life. No one's here to judge." I closed my eyes and took a deep breath, then began reciting the string of threats and swear words I had laid into my attacker. I was a little surprised when not one of them flinched at my choice of colorful words.

A little over half an hour passed before they stopped the recording and shared that they had been trying to capture a serial rapist for the past six months and that he had attacked or raped at least eight women in the Lynnwood area and one in the Edmonds area. Together Detective Jones and Detective Bruce were assigned to track the culprit and felt certain I had captured their man. That made me his tenth victim.

I felt sickened at the thought of anyone else going through the pain, terror and trauma that I had. Nurses, students, coffee shop owners—he had no mercy for any female, age or type. He just searched for the vulnerable and waged his war on their dignity. He was a monster.

Suddenly a disturbing thought entered my head, *Nine! Nine other victims and all the people they have slept with. That's what I have been exposed to!*

I suddenly couldn't get out of there fast enough, I managed to stand, "I have to go now." Detective Jones mumbled something about counseling and I bristled, *Is he crazy? I don't need counseling. I'm a trained rape counselor, I know all about this!*

My response was kind, but firm, "I don't need counseling for this." They both said again that I should consider it. *Yeah, right,* I thought.

The detectives asked us to wait a few moments and left the room, Michelle hugged me and told me I did a good job. I again expressed my embarrassment at my language, but she assured me it was alright.

The detectives returned with Chief of Police, Larry Kalsbeck who took my hand in his, his smile was genuine and he meant well as he said, "You're a hero."

I was horrified.

"No, no! I'm not!" I screamed. I pulled my hand away and turned my back to him. "I just want to congratulate you, we've been trying to get this guy for a long time," he continued. I began to sob and withdrew into the corner of the room. Michelle began to cry as well as she patted my back and told me it was all okay.

Detective Bruce placed his arms around me and buried my head in his chest. I can only imagine the awkward face of the well-meaning chief, "To us you are a real hero," he said as he left the room. I just wanted to escape the hell that had taken over my life. Detective Bruce held me until I could calm down.

Whatever triggered my response would stay with me for a long time. Being labeled a hero was almost as hard as being labeled a victim—I just wanted my life back.

CHAPTER 8 – BACK TO THE SCENE OF THE CRIME

"Family means no one gets left behind or forgotten."
~David Ogden Stiers

We left the police station and Michelle, Jeffery, Lily, Stephanie and I headed back to my townhouse. It was odd, but I had no real feelings about returning to the scene of the worst crime committed against me in my entire life. I was numb, or perhaps still in shock. I felt like some sort of docent, prepared to explain to my children what had happened where—except the rape, I wouldn't get specific about that, and they didn't ask.

We entered and the first thing I noticed was my telephone on the kitchen counter covered in blood. Michelle grabbed a cloth and started to wipe it down, "Don't look, Mom. Let me clean it up."

"It doesn't bother me," I stated and the strange thing was that I meant it. I walked around as if in a trance, I had difficulty finishing sentences and felt completely numb. The feeling was strange and foreign and I wondered if I'd ever be normal again.

I began to search the kitchen cupboards, "They stole it!" I said frantically. I began to shake as I opened one cupboard door after the other, "What?" asked Michelle, "Stole what?"

"The money! It's gone!" I began to shake again.

"Mom," Jeffery tried to calm me, "calm down! What money?" Once again I felt violated, certain I had thrown the money bag inside a cupboard and now it was gone.

"The bag! From the café—the bank bag! It's gone!"

The kids joined in my search, opening drawers and cupboards in a mad effort to track down the receipts. It was as if they felt if they found it, they would help fix all that was wrong.

Somehow Stephanie had the perspicacity to open the dishwasher and there it was. She handed it to me and I unzipped it, the wad of bills was still there and the relief that washed over me was immense, "Oh my God! Oh thank God! They didn't take the money!"

Jeffery and Michelle looked at one another before Jeffery spoke, "Mom, let's get you some clothes. We'll get you over to Mike's, you need to rest." He placed an arm around me and I had the sudden urge to collapse into him and disappear into my grown son's embrace. Perhaps I'd wake up and find it all was just a bad dream—an unthinkable nightmare.

We started toward the stairs and I noticed a part of the wall that had been blown away by one of my bullets, I was much like a bystander, the things I saw registered—the damage to my home, the blood on the floors and walls, the dust where fingerprints had been collected—but I had no feelings about any of it. It was like I was on the outside looking in.

It was difficult to make it up the stairs and Michelle and Jeffery helped me take one step at a time, "Don't look, Mom," said Michelle. I assured them that none of it bothered me and I was telling the truth.

We entered my room and the pool of blood by the bed was still fresh, I heard Stephanie gasp at the sight. "They took my sheets," I said matter-of-factly, "maybe they needed the blood samples."

I saw Michelle look from Stephanie to Jeffery, her face now full of worry. I had watched her expressions morph from anger—to stoic and steadfast—to sadness and now to angst in a matter of hours.

I made my way into the bathroom and noticed the wastebasket full of latex gloves, I surmised they had been used by police to collect evidence and pictured my bedroom a flurry of officers and detectives scavenging for anything to put the monster behind bars for good. When I came out of the bathroom, Mike was there.

He gently embraced me and asked how I was doing and when I would be coming to stay with him. I said it would be within the next few hours and went on to show him and the kids where my battle with the beast had begun, where shots were fired and where we struggled in the hallway.

It didn't occur to me that this was all difficult for them to hear, to me, I was the guide on some haunted trail and they were my tour. Jeffery quickly changed the subject by offering to get sandwiches. I wasn't hungry, or at least I didn't feel hungry—then again I didn't feel anything, only a sharp pain in my chest every time I took a breath.

Michelle, Lily and Stephanie were hungry, so Jeffery said he'd be back with food. Once again relieved to do anything at all to help. Mike left us with a key and told me to come whenever I was ready.

Several minutes later Jeffery called to say not to answer the door, he'd been approached by the press on his way to his car, "He wanted to know all about the lady who'd caught the rapist," he said. "There were at least three satellite trucks from local TV stations parked further down the lot, just stay put."

We'd just hung up with Jeffery when the phone rang again, this time it was Larry, an old friend, inviting me to lunch. I told him I wasn't able because I'd caught the Lynnwood/Edmonds serial rapist and was more than a little battered. He was shocked and after hearing a little of my ordeal, I could tell he was uncomfortable. We hung up and it was only moments before his sister, Barbara, called asking if there was anything she could do to help. I politely declined, assuring her I would be fine.

Michelle called my parents and let them know I was out of the hospital, they offered to have me stay with them, but Michelle politely declined, explaining that I wanted to be close to Caffé Aida and I'd be staying with Mike. They knew Mike well and had his phone number, so they'd know how to reach me.

I headed back to my room to pack a bag, but the fog in my head was thick and I stood in the middle of my room unsure as to what I was to do. I'm not sure how much time had passed when Michelle and Lily came to check on me and I quickly snapped to and remembered why I was up there. I opened a drawer and began gathering items to stuff in a bag, "I'll be right down," I said, but once the girls left me alone, the fog returned and I was suddenly very concerned about my sanity.

I gingerly made my way downstairs and picked up the phone, "Who are you calling?" Michelle asked. I wasn't sure why, but I had an overwhelming urge to phone my dear friends, the Ferraro's.

"Patrick and Carol," I said. Michelle's brow furrowed, "Why now?" she inquired.

"They'll want to know," I answered. She watched me dial and hovered around as I told my friends what had happened and assured them that I was alright. There was something necessary about hearing the familiar and soothing voice of friends. I needed to hear I'd done the right thing by trying to kill a man who violated me so viciously, I needed to hear that my actions were just. It comforted me to hear Carol say, "Right on!" when I told her I aimed to kill.

* * * *

Jeffery returned with sandwiches from a local sub shop and told us that reporters were everywhere, they were knocking on doors and asking other residents questions about the night before. My children shut the blinds in an effort to spare me from any more attacks on my privacy.

There was a knock at the door and Jeffery answered it. It was a newsman inquiring as to my wellbeing and asking if I'd consider an interview. It was clear the word was out that I lived in unit 9. Jeffery politely declined, only stating that I was as well as could be expected and that there would be no interviews for the immediate future. I was grateful my children were protecting me, I didn't want anyone to know who I was.

The press continued to swarm and when Michelle and Stephanie stepped out onto the enclosed balcony for some air, they were spotted and a reporter called out to them, "Did you hear what went on here last night?"

Michelle bristled at the invasion, "You know, you media people have no business being here, especially today!" A mother lion protecting her cubs had nothing on Michelle when it came to guarding her family. If we had stopped to think about it, we may have understood that they were just doing their job, but by now the lack of sleep, shock and trauma had taken their toll.

The media storm continued with frequent knocks at the door until Jeffery put his foot down and declared there would be no interviews and I was no longer in the house. We naively thought that that would be it and once they left I could quietly sneak off to Mike's.

We sat down to eat the sandwiches, which I nibbled to appease my children, and Michelle turned on the TV. It was 11:45am and a news brief came on informing that the Lynnwood/Edmonds serial rapist had been caught. Jeffery jumped up to turn off the television, "Leave it," I said. "Let's watch."

The noon news went into great detail about the last victim had been the one to capture him, they labeled me a hero and I was once again on the outside, looking in—*this could not really have happened. Not to me! I'll wake up soon and it will have all been a nightmare.*

The phone rang again, this time it was my parents saying they had seen the noon report and were proud of me, "Why aren't you at Mike's?" my mother asked. I told her about the gaggle of reporters camped outside wanting an interview and we were unable to leave as a result.

"Madeline, you sure wouldn't want them to know who you are. If you give an interview, every rapist out there will know where to find you."

I felt a twinge of anger at her insensitivity. "I don't think any other rapists will want to fuck with me," I snapped. I was hurt that she was embarrassed by what had happened to her daughter and I ended the conversation quickly, assuring her I was okay and being well taken care of by Jeffery and Michelle.

I hung up the phone and the thought crossed my mind of how present I would be for my own children if such violence had befallen them, but I could think no further than that, I simply didn't have the energy to try and understand her response.

We continued to wait for a window of opportunity to leave the townhouse. Insurance adjusters showed up to assess the damage and Michelle and Stephanie were furious at the intrusion, "Can you give us one day of privacy?" Michelle demanded.

I calmed the girls and explained they were just there to do their job. They adjusters apologized, but continued to go about the business of putting a price on the destruction of my home.

It was the damage they couldn't see that was far more troubling.

CHAPTER 9 – SHELL SHOCKED

"I have this strange feeling none of this is really happening. Like I'm standing far away from myself. Like nothing is real. Have you ever had a feeling like that?"

~A. Manette Ansar

Jeffery offered to take a leave of absence from his job and run my cafe, while Michelle and Lily would take turns chauffeuring me to various appointments until I healed. Jeffery had told the media staked outside that I was no longer at the townhouse, but they were persistent, knocking on the door again and again to inquire as to how I was and would I give an interview. Determined to protect me, again and again Jeffery declined, just assuring them that I was doing as well as could be expected and we would be in touch if I wanted to give an interview.

My landlord came by with the super to access the damage to the home and determine what needed to be repaired. He took one look at me and his eyes filled with tears, "They said no one could possibly reach that window. I should have alarmed it..." I stopped him mid-sentence, "It's not your fault," the look on his face said that no amount of assurance from me was going to make him think otherwise.

They toured the home with Jeffery and left, but not before asking me to please consider returning to live there once the repairs were made. I promised to let them know as soon as I could make a decision, but it wouldn't be for a while, Jeffery gave them his contact information and thanked them for stopping by.

Jeffery saw them to the door and peeked out, he heaved a sigh and turned to me, "They're still out there," he said. "I don't know how we're going to get you out of here without a circus."

"I can't stay here," I was adamant, it was nearly five and would be getting dark soon, for some reason that terrified me.

"We know, Mom, we'll figure it out," he put his arm around me. It felt odd that for so many years I had tended to my children's scraped knees, bruised egos and childhood fears, and now they were caring for me, it would take a while for me to adjust to the tables that had been so violently turned.

"When Detective Jones called earlier I told him about the reporters and he suggested one of you give a brief interview, maybe that will be enough to get them out of here. Once I'm at Mike's, they won't find me." Jeffery and Michelle exchanged glances, but neither made a move for the door—not yet, anyway.

All three local news networks opened with the story of the woman who single handedly nabbed the local serial rapist, local residents were interviewed expressing relief at once again being able to sleep in peace knowing he was behind bars.

A clip of the suspect in the back of a police cruiser played, a blanket over his head. I wondered why in the world they were protecting him—he's an animal! Michelle made a hateful comment at the sight of him, but all I could do was watch.

My chest, face, back and legs throbbed and I just wanted to get out of there and get to Mike's. "That's it," said Jeffery. "I'll give them two minutes." With that he headed out to the barrage of media and gave a short interview. He demanded they not release my name, or that of Jeffery and Michelle and they complied.

He told the reporters of how the suspect had entered my home through a window while I slept, that there was a struggle and that I had been beaten and cut with a knife. He told them how I got hold of my gun and held the man captive until police arrived. They asked if I knew my attacker and Jeffery assured them that I did not, he then asked that they respect my privacy.

Michelle went out and said a few words, mainly that she hoped my attacker would spend the rest of his life in jail. Satisfied, the press dispersed.

I gave Jeffery keys to the townhome and café, gathered some clothes and we headed to Mike's. He was a dear friend, and although we were no longer in a romantic relationship, he showed great compassion and would welcome me with open arms.

A newspaper sat open on Mike's kitchen table. It was the complete story, the twenty-one-year-old suspect had a history of property and petty theft crimes. In at least three of the cases, he had fled the scene when his victim fought back, so women were encouraged to put up a fight while he was on the loose. He lived near the Edmonds Community College.

I read the story, feeling dazed and detached, like I was reading about someone else, not me. Mike, his daughter Gina and I watched the late news that evening after my kids had gone home, they had done all they could do for now and would return in the morning, the news showed the townhome and Jeffery's and Michelle's interviews. *Is that my home? Are those my children? Who did this happen to?*

I couldn't shake the feeling of being immersed in a fog. When the news continued with other local events a man in fatigues with a rifle was shown, I couldn't tell you what the story was about, but the image frightened me. I had a terrible urge to flee the room.

The day had exhausted everyone but me, I'd had less than two hours of sleep in the past twenty-four hours, but I was afraid to close my eyes. It was dark. It had been dark when I was attacked and I was going to be ready this time, I wasn't going to be sound asleep, giving my attacker the opportunity to rape me so viciously—beat me and cut me. *I will never be raped again! Next time—I'll shoot first!*

Gina was the first to excuse herself to bed, Mike helped me off the couch and gave me a prescribed sleeping pill. He asked me where I'd be most comfortable sleeping, on the fold out couch in the family room, or with him. I chose to sleep in his bed with him— that would be the safest.

Mike helped me into bed and told me to wake him if I needed anything. Everything hurt less when I lay flat on the bed, that combined with the sleeping pill and the knowledge that Mike, a tall strong man with a gun near the bed, was beside me must have been the magic formula. By some miracle I drifted off to sleep.

* * * *

I woke early the next morning and I was crying. I didn't know why; I hadn't had a nightmare that I knew of. Mike helped me out of bed and I took the subscribed pills for pain and antibiotics for infection.

I was in a better frame of mind now that it was morning, I was relieved that the days were becoming longer and that meant a good fifteen hours of daylight. I knew that Jeffery and Michelle would return to Mike's before he left for work and I wouldn't be alone. Everyone agreed that it was best for me to have someone close by at all times—at least for now.

My friend Kim called to see how I was doing, she had contacted me the day before and suggested I get in touch with The Center for Counseling in Edmonds, I had declined, but she asked again, and this time I took her up on her offer to call for me. I was beginning to feel out of control and I wasn't quite sure how to get a handle on this new and traumatic twist in my life. Little did I know, life as I knew it would never be the same again.

The morning paper was full of my story, the headline read, "Rape Suspect Tangles with the Wrong Woman!" They identified the suspect as Allan Ray Chesnutt, a twenty-one-year-old restaurant worker from Lynnwood.

Jeffery was quoted, he called me resilient and brave and said they were proud of me for having the presence of mind to hold my attacker. The suspect had been convicted of second degree assault seven years earlier when he attacked a woman with a knife and rifle and served only a few months in a juvenile facility. The article went on to say that if convicted now, he'd face between 52 and 68 years in prison. I read the front section of the paper cover to cover, I had a burning desire to know everything possible about this monster.

Jeffery and Lily arrived and Mike left for work, they asked how I slept and how I was feeling that morning, but I couldn't say. I was still feeling the odd numbness, the only thing I was sure of was my physical pain.

Michelle arrived and Jeffery and Lily left to tend to the café. Michelle made appointments for me for my follow-up medical care. Detective Jones phoned to check up on me and assured us that I had indeed caught the serial rapist, and that was the good news, the bad news was that I was going to need lessons on how to shoot a gun.

It hurt to laugh, but I was thankful for his attempt at humor. He told me it was probably better that I hadn't killed Chesnutt, "You'd probably have a lot more to deal with had you killed him." He went on to tell me a little about some of the other victims; victims whose lives were forever changed. I silently wished I could have killed him before he had a chance to put the other girls through such misery.

Kim showed up with the news that I had a 1pm appointment with The Center for Counseling and offered to drive me there. I wasn't sure what to expect, but I assumed it certainly couldn't hurt to go and perhaps I'd find a way to shake the fogginess I felt submerged in.

My initial interview was with the owner's wife; she asked me to describe my ordeal and I did—verbatim. It was frustrating to me that I couldn't remember details of how to address the daily operation needs of the café to Jeffery, but details of the attack were etched in my brain so vividly.

She listened patiently as I relived the attack. She told me that the owner, Dr. Jantz was not taking any new patients, but considering the severity of my situation, he would see me for the first one or two sessions and get me acclimated to the center and to the idea of the benefits of counseling.

Dr. Jantz was a nice looking man, about fifteen years younger than myself. He had a kind face and a soothing voice and I was instantly comfortable with him. Clipboard in hand, he sat across from me on a small sofa and asked me how I felt, I reiterated that I felt nothing. I was numb and had no real feelings about my experience, except that I was in physical pain.

I had difficulty relaying my thoughts and processing his questions, "Are you angry about what happened to you?" he asked.

"No," I answered, "how can you be angry at an animal?" My answer was honest, I didn't feel anger—I didn't feel anything.

He assured me my mind was taking a break from the trauma and things would return to some sense of normal in time. The remainder of the hour was spent with him asking questions and me attempting to answer in half sentences that seemed to tumble out of my head the moment I began them. I was frustrated and afraid.

I managed to relay my fears to Dr. Jantz; I was afraid of the dark, of falling asleep, I was afraid of being recognized in the community.

"I'll never put the top of my convertible down again."

"Why?" Dr. Jantz asked. "Because, I don't want to be seen," I answered. "I want to hide in a place where no one ever mentions what occurred that night again."

I told him my fear of contracting AIDS from the rapist and that I'd have to wait at least three months before I could take my first test—"Three agonizing months!" That test would only be followed with more.

Dr. Jantz advised me to take it one day at a time and gave me the name of a physician he recommended, Dr. Leslie Newton. He let me know my counseling and medical bills would be covered under Crime Victims Compensation and that between that and my own insurance I wouldn't have to worry about that. He said he'd like to see me the following morning and told me he'd make the initial appointment with Dr. Newton on my behalf.

I left the office with Kim and she asked if I'd mind if she made a quick stop on the way back to Mike's. I really just wanted to get back to my children, but she had been kind to take me, so I said it would be okay.

I opted to stay in the car while she ran into a local business, it was only for a few minutes, but I began to panic and hyperventilate. By the time she returned I was desperate to get back to Mike's, she asked if I'd like to stop for lunch, but I refused, "Please, just get me back to my children," I begged.

When we got to Mike's, Michelle was waiting for me. She had spent the afternoon setting up doctor appointments that would work with her schedule since I was unable to drive. She suggested I rest, but I couldn't relax enough to sleep. Mike returned from work and Kim and Michelle both left, with Michelle promising to return in the morning.

Mike and I sat on the couch and talked about what a sadistic animal Chesnutt was. Then he blindsided me, "You probably liked it."

I felt like I'd been punched in the stomach, "Mike! That's not even funny!" I was terribly hurt by his insensitivity and he knew it, "You know I was only kidding," he tried to laugh it off. Mike and I had a history of kidding around during our time as a couple, but this wasn't the time for jokes. "I'm sorry," he said. I just wanted to go to bed and he helped me off the couch and I took a sleeping pill and my antibiotic and we went to bed.

I was angry at his remark, and oddly—it felt good to feel something.

CHAPTER 10 –THE NEW NORMAL

"I was happier before, when I lead a normal life."
~Enrique Iglesias

The story in the Saturday paper quoted Sergeant Greg Wean, "The suspect has admitted to raping the woman and was actually glad to see the officers when they arrived seconds after her call to nine-one-one."

I realized that Allan Chesnutt must have thought I was going to kill him. Had I known about the last bullet, I would have—he lucked out.

The flowers and get well wishes began to arrive; it seemed everyone from the local gas station, to the bank where I made my daily deposits was wishing me a speedy recovery. My parents sent a card that read, "Do keep us apprised of the developments regarding the scumbag!"

My employees sent a message that they hoped to see me back at the shop soon, and Michelle and Gabe, her boyfriend at the time, sent flowers along with a handwritten note assuring me that, "Everything will be just fine."

Customers from the coffee shop sent flowers and gifts that let me know I was missed at my place at the coffee shop. I was often the first face they'd see in the morning, and my absence was noted, "Take the time you need, but know you are in our thoughts and prayers."

People in the community that I didn't even know reached out to say, "Thank you for making Edmonds a safer place for all of us." They wanted to meet me, have lunch with me and in some way bask in the power I had exercised over my attacker

I was inundated with mail from childhood friends, distant relatives—even Mike's ex-wife sent a card. That surprised me greatly as I knew she didn't care for me, I was Mike's first long-term girlfriend after their divorce and that squelched any chance of them reconciling. I later found out there had been some talk of them getting back together, but when I came into the picture, all that went out the window. I did make certain that Mike was divorced, even going as far as to ask to see the divorce decree—I was not going to be involved with a married man.

Her card was kind and compassionate, she and Mike's daughters wished me strength for a full recovery and said they were "proud" of me for my courage during such a difficult time. I read the card over and over, grateful for their wishes and amazed at their compassion. While Mike and his ex-wife couldn't make their marriage work, they did raise two kind and loving daughters. I had a great deal of respect for that.

Suffice it to say, I was having a difficult time embracing the celebrity that came with surviving a tragedy. While the kindness was appreciated, I would have done anything to have my life back.

* * * *

The first day after the attack went quickly, Mike's Italian heritage shone through as he put out food and made certain everyone had plenty to eat. That seemed to be a go-to for Italians—food meant comfort and healing. My mother was the same way.

I took a sleeping pill that had been prescribed by my physician and I was grateful for the aid in falling asleep. Otherwise, I was in a hyper-vigilant, but foggy state. I walked around Mike's place in a zombie-like state, feeling only the physical pains of the fight.

My parents, along with my sister and brother-in-law arrived Sunday afternoon and my mother's eyes welled when she saw me. It was clear she hadn't expected me to look so physically battered. They all hugged me gently, so as to not hurt me any worse than I already was. My mother, sister and I went into the bedroom and I lifted my shirt to show the knife wounds, bruises and burns on my back, arms and legs. My broken toe caused me to walk with a limp and my face was black and blue, the results of my attack were more than obvious.

I climbed into my dad's lap, something I hadn't done since I was a child. I took comfort in his arms and would have spent the day there had they not asked to see the townhome. I had no desire to go there, so Michelle and Jeffery agreed to drive them over, while I stayed behind.

There's something so innate about returning to the scene of the crime. Anyone who desires to do it knows the experience won't be pleasant, they know the place will be haunted with the ghosts of a victim's innocence, wellbeing and assurance that bad things don't happen to good people. That assumption went right out the window when Chesnutt dared to climb through it.

But people go back, they stare at the remnants of a struggle and try and piece the moments of terror together. Why? I may never fully understand, but it seems to be in our DNA. Crosses on the side of the road mean that someone returned to see the exact spot their loved one left this world. Blinded by the diamonds of window-shield fragments in the noon-day sun, they search for any trace of the soul they lost. Searching for reason amongst the rubble must be a way of quieting our hurt, anger and inability to comprehend—loss.

Unless one is a trained detective, rarely is anything taken away from a trip to the scene of the crime, other than the affirmation that, yes, bad things really do happen to good people, and perhaps that knowledge should make us a little afraid.

When they returned, Mom was visibly upset. The bloodstained walls and carpeting were too much for her. I hugged her and assured her not to worry, those leftovers of that treacherous night only served to remind me that I had survived the ordeal. I didn't realize at the time that I had quickly become a pro at burying my feelings about the horrific occurrence.

After lunch, my sister Aileen offered to take me to an appointment with a plastic surgeon the following morning to determine if my nose had been fractured or broken, now that some of the swelling had subsided. I wanted any visible reminders of that night to be attended to as quickly as possible.

That evening, after everyone had left, Mike and I spent a quiet evening in front of the television. I tried to push his comment from

Friday night out of my mind, but it had a tendency of creeping back in and I'd feel the hurt and anger bubble up. I took a sleeping pill to quiet my head and let me sleep. Miraculously, it worked.

* * * *

On Monday morning, Mike went to work. I didn't mind being alone for a short time in the daylight and even thought Puka hadn't been any help on the night of the attack, having her there with me gave me comfort.

The police had found her curled up on the floor, sleeping near the foot of the bed. She apparently bit one of the officers when they tried to awaken her and that surprised me, Puka had never bitten anyone before. While the officer was fine and didn't require stitches, I wondered why her attack mode surfaced after the assault and not during; my vet later surmised that either Chesnutt drugged her, or she was paralyzed with fear during the ordeal and unable to move. Either way, I felt awful that Chesnutt's actions affected my adorable dog, as well as me.

Calls and inquiries continued to filter in, my employees told me that my favorite clients, Scott and Cindy had asked about me. They were a lovely couple, and I considered them my most loyal customers, starting their morning with a cup of my coffee and often returning two or three times a day. They had been living together for a few years and had six children between them. I often admired their mutual respect and obvious love for one another.

I loved all my customers, but Scott and Cindy were special. I called Cindy at her office and she expressed how awful she and Scott felt and asked where I was staying. I told her I was at my ex-boyfriend's house, not far from the business. We arranged for her to stop by the following day as Monday was already busy with an appointment with Dr. Jantz as well as the visit to the plastic surgeon.

Aileen picked me up and we grabbed a quick lunch at a local restaurant. It felt odd to be out and about, as if all was right with the world. I looked around and watched as locals scanned menus. Waitresses stood with pens at the ready to get the orders just so; *dressing on the side, easy on the mayo, can I get that on whole wheat?*

I silently wondered when my life would be that simple again. *Would it ever?* Or had that horrific bastard robbed me of ever having my biggest dilemma be weather to have my turkey sandwich on rye or pumpernickel.

Aileen snapped me out of my thoughts with casual conversation, I felt envious that she could carry on with her life, she was in control and organized and I felt befuddled and clumsy. My equilibrium and sense of balance was off due to trauma to my body, but also to my soul.

* * * *

Dr. Jantz was warm and welcoming, I told him about the Sunday visit with my family and he asked me how it had gone, I shrugged and said, "I don't know." That was the truth, I had no feeling about the visit or my family's reaction to my attack. I felt strangely empty and unable to tap into any feelings—my insides were numb. He insisted I see his colleague, Dr. Taylor, and I agreed to an appointment the following day.

We said our goodbyes and Aileen drove me to Valley General Hospital in Renton to the plastic surgeon's office. When we entered the office, two women behind the desk seemed to know who I was and why I was there. They ushered me into the examining room and my wait for my doctor was minimal.

He examined my nose and assured me it wasn't broken; only swollen. He had been my doctor years before and had repaired my nose to correct two botched surgeries that had been performed by an ear, nose and throat doctor. I trusted him when he said to leave it alone and allow it to heal on its own.

After my last surgery, I had been told to minimalize activity that might cause impact to my nose; no more waterskiing or contact sports that might risk a blow to the face. Although my breathing was labored due to the swelling, and I was still having great difficulty moving through my pain, I was a little relieved that I wouldn't have to endure surgery to repair my nose, I would, however have to be patient as it healed on its own and that meant avoiding mirrors as much as possible. They only served to remind me of Chesnutt.

When I returned to the lobby, the nurses had congregated and were waiting for me.

"We just want to thank you," said one of the women, "you're a real hero to us."

I suddenly panicked, I couldn't get out of there fast enough, I managed curt, "thanks", and Aileen and I quickly left. She helped me into the car and I felt compelled to explain to her how it bothered me when anyone would bring up Chesnutt, or my new and sudden celebrity of "local hero."

"I don't know these people, Aileen, and they certainly don't know me." I sensed she was having difficulty understanding my aversion to the attention from strangers; we rode in silence back to Mike's house, I thanked my sweet sister and she left.

* * * *

Michelle arrived a little later and told me she had gone to the courtroom where Allan Chesnutt was arraigned. Detective Jones from Edmonds and Detective Bruce from Lynwood were both there and they insisted she sit between them during the proceeding.

"I think they were concerned I was going to do something, the way they flanked me." She later told me she had taken a gun to the courtroom, she had purchased it after the attack and put it in her purse, then had forgotten she had it with her.

Later that evening Jeffery, Stephanie and Michelle's boyfriend, Gabe stopped by and we watched the 5:00 news. They talked about the arraignment and the "woman" who had captured the culprit, making the streets and bedrooms of local women safe again.

Jeffery had been in touch with much of the local media, as they had his contact info and cell number. They requested interviews with me and Jeffery served as my guardian-angel-buffer, telling them he would let them know when, and if, I was up to it. He was especially impressed with one reporter from the Seattle Post-Intelligencer named Darrell Glover and promised him the first interview, with my permission, should I ever decide to give one.

The kids left a little later and I felt the same anxiety that I had in previous nights after the sun set. I tried to distract myself with other matters and occurred to me that I had ordered two tickets to the Seattle Sonics playoff game against Houston the following evening, my friend Brock was to deliver them to the café the next morning. I knew Mike would love to go, he watched the Sonics on television whenever he could, so he jumped at my invitation. Good, I thought, something to look forward to. I took my sleeping pill and we went to bed.

* * * *

The next morning, I got a call from Detective Jones telling me that the police were called to the townhome to break up the media circus that had formed there. Satellite trucks were everywhere and reporters continued to knock on doors in search of me. It was clear the neighbors were growing tired of the commotion and wanted their privacy back.

He said that a reporter from CNN, along with several local reporters, had been to the department in search of information and had requested the 911 tape, which Detective Jones refused to give out. I thanked him for protecting my identity. He went on to say that the Snohomish County Prosecuting Attorney, David Kurtz, was planning a meeting with all the victims in order to explain what they could expect in the coming days regarding the court procedures. I declined to be a part of that, but Detective Jones reminded me that it was early and perhaps I should think about it and we could talk about it again at a later time.

A little later, Detective Bruce called and told me that some of the other victims were interested in meeting with me, to thank me.

"NO!" I was adamant, "I don't want anyone to thank me. I did nothing that anyone in my position wouldn't have done, given the chance. I don't want to meet them."

I think Detective Bruce was taken aback at my response, and I could barely explain my reaction to myself, let alone him. I would later figure out that facing my fellow victims would just be acknowledging that I did, in fact, get attacked by this animal. He encouraged me to go to the meeting with Prosecuting Attorney Kurtz and I promised to give it some thought. Both officers knew I was in counseling and were glad I had decided to seek it early, they assured me that counseling is what helped the other survivors cope thus far.

Counseling or not, something felt immeasurably unfair to me; myself, along with the other victims, were allowed to become broken; in need of repair because a monster had walked the streets of our quiet town. We were forced to deal with the anger, grief, fear and guilt of being brutally attacked. Although the help we would receive would be covered monetarily, we lost something that was irreplaceable—our sense of safe.

One hideous creature did so much damage, trickling down from his ten victims and into the lives of their friends and loved ones where it continued to spread from there—the steps to pick up all the broken pieces were impossible to count.

* * * *

In the days following, newspaper articles would state that Chesnutt was charged with eight counts of first degree rape and one count of first degree burglary. I felt he should have been charged with attempted murder in my case and this caused me to wonder about our justice system.

I had had a change of heart and decided I would meet with Dave Kurtz the following Friday. I wanted to tell him my thoughts on this demented rapist and the charges leveled against him.

Jeffery was quoted in the papers saying, "She was cut numerous times, he threatened to snap her neck—to kill her. She's hopeful the charges will be increased." The article went on to say that I was attempting to deal with the psychological fallout from the attack and Jeffery went on to say, "She can't yet comprehend that this has happened to her, she feels as though it were someone else. I'm not sure the reality has sunk in."

Jeffery's instincts were right on mark, I felt I was living a surreal dream. I was transported out of my secure, naïve, happy life in an instant and now I had to deal with the reality of a future, where I carried with me the knowledge that the world was a strange, scary and unsafe place—and there was no place to go to escape it.

Cindy came over with the gift of a gold angel and a card that read,

Dearest Madeline,
Our thoughts are with you always.
Please call on us anytime.
With love, your friends, Scott & Cindy

She told me that Scott would love to see me and asked if I'd like to take a ride as he was working on a house not far from Mike's. It sounded like a good idea, the day was warm and I could use the fresh air.

When Scott saw me, he embraced me warmly. His eyes welled as he told me how sorry he was. He gave me his pager number and told me to never hesitate to call if I needed anything at all. Their heartfelt sincerity was touching, I felt cared for when I was around these lovely people. Cindy and I left and she drove me back to Mike's where I would find Michelle and Jeffery waiting to take me to my first appointment with Dr. Taylor at The Center for Counseling. Jeffery had remembered to bring the tickets for the Sonics game and I only hoped I could maintain the energy to go.

Dr. Taylor was an older gentleman, but it was clear from his physique that he took great care of himself. I had been instructed to bring my prescriptions with me so that he would know what I was taking.

We settled into chairs and he asked me how I was doing, "I'm fine except for the chest pain and trying to walk with a broken toe," I said, "but I'm getting better with each day."

"What about the anger?" he asked, his brow knit with concern.

I told him it was futile to be angry, "He was an animal. How can you be angry at an animal? An animal doesn't know better."

I could tell my answer stumped him, I'm sure he had had other patients that had been violated who would have jumped at the chance to spill their anger all over his spotless white carpet, but I couldn't see the point. He gestured toward a chair,

"Pretend Allan Chesnutt is in that chair, what would you like to say to him?"

"Nothing," I said, "I have nothing to say to him."

"Try this," he said and turned his own chair to face the empty one where supposedly Allan Chesnutt sat; his voice boomed, "How dare you come into my safe home—rape me and threaten to kill me!" He then asked me to try.

"I have no desire to say anything to him, I have no feelings about 'it' or him."

The whole idea seemed silly to me.

I'm sure I left Dr. Taylor frustrated in his desire to help me and my inability to cooperate, not out of spite—but rather, a lack of energy toward the entire situation. At that point, I just wanted to go back to Mike's.

I thanked Dr. Taylor and assured him I was bruised and battered, but otherwise okay and ready to get on with the rest of my life. Something I truly believed, if I could just get past the physical reminders of the rape; the bruises, the pain, the broken toe—then I could put this nightmare behind me move on. It was the epitome of wishful thinking.

* * * *

That evening was the Sonic's game I had invited Mike to and I decided to go. I showered and put on my make-up, covering the visuals as best I could. That was the first time I'd put on makeup since the attack and it made me feel better to look in the mirror and see something of my familiar face looking back at me. I remember thinking, maybe no one will even suspect...

Mike drove us to an Italian restaurant near the Coliseum to grab a bite before the game, I still had no appetite and picked at my meal before we noticed the time and knew we had to head to the game if we didn't want to miss the tip off.

I walked much slower than usual due to the pain and had to stop several times as we made our way on foot from the restaurant to the Coliseum. The shortness of breath made it impossible to walk at our normally brisk pace and a few times, I thought we would never get there.

We eventually made it and found our seats, which were great! I could always depend on Brock to ensure my Sonics seats were prime. It was a sold-out crowd of screaming fans who jumped to their feet in a constant effort to cheer the Sonics on to victory.

I was usually one of those fans, but not tonight. Tonight I could barely breathe in a seated position, the pain combined with the heat generated by thousands of fans was too much at times and I had to make my way, with Mike's help, into the cooler, less populated area near the refreshment stands until I could catch my breath.

Back in our seats, I looked around and could hardly remember being one of them, the enthusiastic, carefree followers of our pro Seattle team—it was just another part of my new normal.

At some point during the game the reader board flashed, "Welcome Madeline!"

I'm no one special, I thought, *how could those words possibly be referring to me?*

CHAPTER 11 – THE OVERDOSE

"The flashbacks can happen anytime, anywhere. I never know what might trigger me. It's like walking on tombstones. I'm tired."

~Unknown

Man arrested in rapes, 'numb', his lawyer says, but he is aware of what's going on. He is having to face reality. The line was from an article in The Seattle Post-Intelligencer and written by Darrell Glover. He quoted Jeffery, who stated that I was doing as well as could be expected. He went on to say that I was under the care of a psychiatrist to cope with the psychological trauma and finished with my disappointment that Chesnutt wouldn't be charged with attempted murder.

Kurtz was quoted as saying that there was not enough evidence of intent to murder since Chesnutt had not attempted murder on any of his previous victims. I found that argument weak, but had little idea of how to demand the additional charge, or the energy to pursue it.

When I'd read these articles, I'd come away 'numb', too. Just like Chesnutt's lawyer had described him. I was often asked how I was feeling and could rarely come up with anything more than, "Okay"—it's difficult to describe how you're feeling, when you have none.

On Thursday, May 20th, one week after the attack, I woke early, dressed and headed for the victims' meeting with David Kurtz at the Snohomish County Courthouse. Michelle, Jeffery and Lily accompanied me, my broken toe and resulting slow pace caused us to be five minutes late. I began to have trouble breathing as we approached the conference room. I could see the backs of the heads of my fellow victims as they had been seated at the table before me. Detective Bruce and Detective Jones stood on either side of the entry. I stopped in my tracks.

"I don't want to go in!" I began to cry as panic seemed to take over, "I don't want anyone to look at me or say anything to me." Detective Bruce placed his arm around my shoulder and said, "You'll be okay. Just catch your breath, you don't have to go in right away."

They sat us in an area outside the conference room until I could regain my composure and then, with Michelle and Jeffery flanking me, we entered the room and were seated on a long sofa against the wall.

David Kurtz introduced himself, as Prosecuting Attorney, he went on to explain the judicial process we could expect. He told us that Chesnutt had confessed to the attacks and had given statements that would corroborate our own. He explained what would occur if the case went to trial, which it would if Chesnutt pleaded not guilty, but they expected that he would plead guilty and in that case, there would be no trial.

I tuned out Dave Kurtz and looked around the room at my fellow victims, they ranged in age from eighteen to late thirties; all attractive, either students or professionals, all having nothing in common with the others in the room, except that they had been terrorized by Allan Chesnutt.

One girl with long dark hair continually turned to me with tears in her eyes. She brought out the maternal side of me and I later found out she was the youngest of Chesnutt's victims and had been brutalized for nearly four hours.

A handful of the victims asked questions concerning sentencing and how long Chesnutt would be put away, I listened to their voices and wondered what hell Chesnutt had put them through. I felt a kindred connection with each victim. As if we were all unwilling participants in some tragic novel. A connection none of us ever asked for, but here we were, brought together by a monster.

Questions arose about overcrowded jails resulting in an early release for Chesnutt, Kurtz assured us that due to the severity of Chesnutt's crimes, that was highly unlikely. I noticed that he didn't use the word, "impossible", we would have to be satisfied with "highly unlikely." I found that troubling.

With no death sentence, and only the punishment of jail-time, Chesnutt could one day be back on the street. If he were dead, I wouldn't have to worry. He would never come back. That's what I wanted, assurance that this man would never—ever, have the chance to hurt us again.

I drifted into a fog; I could hear questions being asked, and Dave's voice responding, but the content was no longer registering. I could hear Jeffery's voice as he asked a question, but couldn't make out the response, I saw him jot something in the black calendar book in which he kept notes and reminders. I watched as the others began to rise and realized it must be time to go.

I stood and two of the victims approached me, "I just want to say thank you," said one. I wanted to put my hands over my ears and shout, "I don't want to hear this! This is why I didn't want to be here!" But I didn't, I somehow managed to politely respond with, "You would have done the same thing had you been given the chance."

They all began to gather around me, my children stayed close, insulating me from the barrage of praise that they knew I couldn't handle. While the victims were kind, my children knew I could fall apart at any moment and they were determined that that would not happen.

The youngest with the long brown hair hugged me and we both cried. As we left the conference room and headed down the hall, another victim's fiancé sidled up. His fiancé was several strides ahead with Jeffery, probably engaged in conversation about the sentencing.

"I heard you were a rape counselor," he said. His delivery was shy and it came on the heels of praise for my "heroic" efforts in capturing the attacker.

"Do you think..." he paused and then continued, "she enjoyed it?"

The shock had obviously registered in my expression, because he quickly followed his question with, "I sometimes think she did, like maybe, she likes all the attention."

I swallowed hard, trying to allow the counselor in me to surface, this young man was obviously confused and nearly as affected by the experience as his fiancé. The violation, the guilt, the inability to rescue her at her direst hour—all personal failures on his part, according to him.

"No. I can tell you in no uncertain terms that she did not enjoy anything about what happened to her." I knew from my training that many men thought that women had a secret fantasy of being raped. This was ignorance in its truest form.

"She needs your love and support now more than ever," I insisted. He went on to say that sometimes she wanted to talk about it and he couldn't and other times he wanted to talk about it and she shut down. I told him those incidents were completely normal, that he should be prepared to listen when she did open up—it was her cry for comfort and part of the healing process. I listened to myself speak the words, but was dumbfounded that I couldn't possibly apply them to my own situation. I was shut down and couldn't imagine ever returning to my former, communicative, insightful self.

He thanked me for my advice and seemed reassured. I could only hope he could provide the support she needed, but at that moment, I had little in the way of optimism. We said our goodbyes and headed to our cars.

* * * *

The Seattle Post-Intelligencer started the morning of May 20th with a report that Chesnutt had admitted to raping eight women and assaulting two others over a six-month period. His details of the attacks were consistent with his victims' accounts and he confessed to using his mother's kitchen knives in his first four assaults and a gun in at least four subsequent assaults. He had moved to the Edmonds area from Tacoma, Washington shortly before the rapes began to take place. He'd lived with his mother and worked as a dishwasher at the Family Pancake House on Highway 99 in Edmonds. While it was less than a mile from the café, I had never been to the restaurant.

Jeffery was again quoted on my condition, "It's up and down a lot—nighttime's are really hard. I don't think she sleeps well."

Chesnutt's apartment was searched and turned up damaging evidence. His blood sample matched that of blood found at the scene of a rape that occurred on November 4, 1992, in that attack the suspect cut his hand and bled on the victim's nightshirt.

They found clothing that had been stolen from one of his victim's apartment and a glove that matched one that was found in the condo of a woman attacked on December 17, 1992. They found steak knives, CO_2 cartridges and a green hooded sweatshirt that fit the description of one worn by an attacker who raped a woman in her Lynnwood home on March 2nd, 1993. All arrows pointed to Chesnutt as the one terrorizing the community.

On May 20th, the Seattle Times editorial section mentioned me and my encounter with Chesnutt more than once. The Brady Bill was becoming a hot topic and the rebuttals in response to an editorial supporting it were loud and clear in favor of the right to own a firearm;

"Your May 14th editorial, 'Chipping at the Edges of America's Culture', seems to ignore your page one story, "Guile and a Gun got Suspect in Lynnwood Rapes." A woman with a GUN saved her own life, provided a public service and did what the police department has, so far, been unable to do; capture a suspected serial rapist. If your editors had their way, she would not have had a gun."

The letters to the editor were adamant that my access to a firearm not only saved me, but aided me in apprehending a criminal who would surely have raped again, had it not been for my ability to legally own a gun.

My Second Amendment rights had never occurred to me, until now. I realized that my right to own a firearm had saved my life and served in getting a criminal off the street. To this day I do not believe I would be here to share my story had it not been for my right to own a gun.

* * * *

My children took me back to Mike's, the meeting with the other victims still fresh. I assured them that I would be fine until Mike returned home. I knew they had their own lives to attend to and I was feeling a little guilty about shifting their focus in recent days, and hurried them on their way.

It wasn't long before it became dark and I began feeling nervous about being alone. I picked up the phone in search of a friendly voice, Jeffery and I visited for a few minutes, he was always a good listener, but I knew he had a full plate with his own life and now the café. I feigned interest in how the business was doing, but in reality, I was just thankful for the voice on the other end of the phone. We made plans to have lunch the following day and hung up.

Mike arrived home and by this time, I was agitated and afraid. I told him I would appreciate if he would call and let me know when he was going to be gone so long. That way I could make plans with friends, anything to squelch the noise of being alone.

He wasn't happy with my complaint, he had been meeting with clients and wasn't used to a curfew. He disappeared into his office and I went into the family room. I sat on the sofa and the day played out before me, suddenly I saw all of Chesnutt's victims, I registered the faces that were in the conference room earlier that day, they were young, older, pretty, plain—the one thing they had in common was Allan Chesnutt. He had terrorized us all.

Suddenly, without warning, my heart began to race. I broke into a feverish sweat; I was back to the fight of my life. "Shut up! Shut up! We're going to kill you!" He held a knife to my back and threatened to break my neck. It was happening all over again, exactly like before and I was terrified. I began to sob.

Panicked, I jumped to my feet and headed to Mike's kitchen, the pills prescribed to me were right there on the counter and I downed every one of the sleeping pills. They usually took a good thirty minutes to work, but I needed them to work now!

I couldn't stand that I was being attacked again! I was willing the pills to work fast, I knew I'd be okay in the morning, but for now I needed the escape to sleep. I went back into the family room and sat on the hide-a-bed. He straddled my back and twisted my neck.

I reached for the phone and dialed Michelle, I just wanted to hear a familiar voice. I felt like such a burden. I had always been so capable—so independent, and this was foreign to me. When I divorced Tom, I vowed to make it on my own and I was proud to have accomplished just that. I hadn't asked my parents for help as many I knew had resorted to, but here I was dependent on my children to do everything for me. I felt crippled and robbed of the independence I had earned.

Michelle's voice was groggy; it was clear I had awakened her. I was crying as told her it was happening all over again. "Mom, it's okay. It's a flashback. Where's Mike?"

She asked to speak to Mike, but I told her I was reluctant to bother him, "Mom, you're slurring your words, what's going on? How many pills did you take?" Her voice became panicked, "Get Mike! I want to talk to him!"

I was adamant that I didn't want to bother him, "No, I don't want to bother him." She begged off and hung up, "I'll call you back." I cried as the phone went silent, "Okay," I said.

The terrifying thoughts continued to seep into my brain, it was happening to me all over again. The phone rang and I picked it up, I was still sobbing.

"Hello," I said, it was Michelle. "Mom, please get Mike for me!"

"I just want it to stop!" I cried.

"How many, Mom? How many pills?"

I felt a sudden wave of peace washing over me, it was warm and welcoming, I felt good, "I don't know, one or—maybe...two." I was tired; so very tired.

I woke up in the emergency room. The first faces I saw were those of Officer L.P. Miller, the first responder on the night of the attack, and Sergeant Debbie Smith, who was not only there on that dreadful night, but she stayed with me afterward in the emergency room. They were at the foot of the gurney I had been placed on. Their expressions were sad and I started to cry as I came to. A nurse had been attempting to wake me up. Sergeant Smith came around to the side of the gurney and took my hand.

"I had a flashback," I managed, "it was so real. It was happening all over again—I just wanted it to stop."

Her voice was reassuring, "I know. It's okay, it wasn't real."

She cupped my hand in both of hers and her skin felt soft and warm, "Are you seeing a counselor?"

I nodded, "Yes, at the Center for Counseling..." Before I had a chance to say his name, Jeffery and Lily walked in. They looked relieved to see me, but they looked tired and bewildered.

"Are you okay?" Jeffery's look of concern made me once again feel like our roles had been reversed. I assured them I was okay, and the nurse gave me an awful black drink that looked and tasted like coal.

"It will make her better," she told Jeffery, "just make sure she doesn't go back to sleep for a few hours. Does she have an appointment anytime soon with her counselor?"

"Yes," said Jeffery, "this afternoon."

I was released in the care of Jeffery and Lily and they asked if I'd like to stay at their home for a while, I declined, I wanted to stay in Edmonds and be near the café. I think I felt that somehow it gave me some form of control in an otherwise uncontrollable situation, besides, I was nervous about being without my pills.

I was hungry to feel something, anything. I had lost my ability to feel anything other than physical pain after the attack.

I began to think about my former self; the confident business woman intent on success. The more money I made, the more money I wanted to make. The more material things I possessed, the more I wanted. I spent less time with family and friends and instead spent my days planning my next steps in a world of spreadsheets and proposals to expand my business.

Material things had become important to me and now, suddenly possessions meant nothing to me. I would look at the beautiful furnishings I had collected over the years and think, so what? Who cares?

I no longer did. I learned from the life threatening attack that you can possess all the riches in the world and in the end they mean nothing. Making money would never again be the most important thing in my life.

While my children meant more to me than money, I hadn't been spending much time with them since I had been on my own. Now, knowing how quickly life could be over, I wanted to enjoy them more than ever.

I was no longer impressed by what people owned, or how much they had in the bank. I began to realize that those who had a lot of "things", often weren't very nice people. Possessions meant nothing when it came to character, empathy and kindness.

The attack did far more than leave me with visible bruises and broken bones, for better or worse, it changed me in how I viewed the world.

'

CHAPTER 12 – THE WILL TO RECOVER

"You can get a monkey off your back, but the circus never leaves town."
~*Anne Lammott*

Once back at Mike's, I immediately called Dr. Newton's office to get a refill on my sleeping pills. The nurse I spoke to asked my name and put me on hold, it was only a moment before Dr. Newton picked up, "Madeline, I can't refill your prescription. I was advised about what happened last night."

I was stunned, news traveled fast and it wasn't even accurate, "I wasn't trying to kill myself," I pleaded, "I was having a flashback."

"I'm sorry," he said, "I wouldn't feel comfortable prescribing anything like that again," I understood his position and felt bad for putting him in such a quandary.

He told me my HIV test had come back negative and that he would pray for me, I was well aware that it would take at least three months before we could determine if I was indeed free of the virus, but I thanked him and hung up.

I was scheduled to meet with the Victim/Witness Counselor for the Snohomish County Prosecuting Attorney that morning at 11:00. She was to keep all Chesnutt's victims informed on the developments in the case. I called and told her I wasn't up to the meeting that morning, she seemed to know what had happened the night before, How was news traveling so fast? I told her about the flashback and accidental overdose, "I was just trying to get some sleep," I explained. She was kind and we rescheduled the appointment, "Call me anytime," she offered.

* * * *

Later that afternoon Jeffery took me to my appointment with Dr. Jantz. He had already heard about my flashback and subsequent visit to the ER. He advised me that Michelle had reservations about my staying with Mike and asked why I hadn't gone to Mike in my panicked state, "I didn't want to bother him," I said.

"I wasn't sure he would understand." How could he? I didn't understand myself what was happening. Dr. Jantz explained that the flashbacks were normal, and one way to deal with them was to talk my way out of the nightmare. I was to tell myself, "This is not happening," he advised me to find something in the room, like a lamp, and touch it, saying, "This is a lamp, this is real, the flashback isn't."

"Don't be afraid of the flashback," said Dr. Jantz, "it's the mind's way of remembering." He told me that many people who live through life and death situations experience flashbacks. I asked how long I might expect to experience them and he told me that he had patients that served in Viet Nam and still had flashbacks, but with time they would likely become fewer and fewer.

He inquired about my dreams, I told him I didn't recall any, but twice I had woken up crying. He said I had likely had a dream about the attack, but lacked the ability to recall the dream. He said in time I'd remember the dreams, when I could, "handle it."

I didn't want to waste one more second in the past, I wanted to forget it ever occurred, but he was adamant that I be in the company of someone who would be available to me. I insisted I was fine at Mike's and his place was in close proximity to my café, "I want to be close to my business."

Jeffery was waiting for me when the visit was over and he drove me back to Mike's and asked if I was okay to be alone. I told him I was and he left to run errands for the café. Detective Bruce called and asked if he could stop by and see me, I gave him Mike's address and was actually grateful for the expected company.

He arrived shortly after and we sat down at the dining room table, he was aware of the night before and asked me how I was doing.

"I'm fine," I said, "I wasn't trying to kill myself," I was beginning to grow tired of defending my need to escape the horror of the flashback in any way possible.

"You're not dealing with this," he said gently.

"What do you mean?" I asked, unsure how one "deals" with that kind of vicious attack.

"You're very matter-of-fact about the ordeal, have you cried?"

"A little...but honestly, what good is crying going to do? It happened. A good cry isn't going to make that go away."

He told me he thought I had a lot to cry about, what he didn't understand was I couldn't even muster up the feeling necessary to cry. Most of the time, I still felt nothing.

"Why don't you get out of town for the weekend?" He suggested.

"I have nowhere to go," I responded.

"How about the ocean? It's a peaceful place, take a friend with you."

"My friends are all married or have boyfriend," I said, completely dismissing the idea as impossible.

Just then there was a knock on the door, it was Scott, after giving me a gentle hug, I introduced him to Detective Bruce.

"I was just telling Madeline that I think it would be good for her to get out of town for the weekend. Scott agreed.

"I really don't have anyone to ask with this late notice," I said.

Scott's brow shot north, "Why not Cindy? She'd love to go. She could use a break, too. It'd be perfect."

He promised to have Cindy call me and left.

I was surprised he offered Cindy's time so easily, I knew how busy they both were; constantly running here, or there, to meet clients, discuss proposals or give estimates. Both of their businesses were booming and that combined with six kids, all going off in different directions made them far busier than I ever was and I couldn't imagine it would be easy to drop everything and head out of town for the weekend. I came to the understanding that it wouldn't be easy, but they had become more than kind customers who frequented my café, they had become genuine, caring friends.

After Scott left, Detective Bruce brought up the arraignment that was scheduled for Monday, May 24th. He asked if I was planning to be there and I told him I was, along with Michelle and Jeffery. He squirmed just a little before asking his next question, "Where's your gun?"

I confirmed that I had brought it with me to Mike's. "May I keep it for you?" he asked, "I'll lock it up in my locker at work until you want it back."

Without verbalizing it, I knew he was trying to protect me from myself, if another flashback occurred, I might become desperate enough to go for the weapon. I nodded and went to the bedroom to get it.

I handed it to Detective Bruce and he assured me I could have it back whenever I wanted. I didn't tell him that Mike also had a gun in the house and that I knew where he kept it. I didn't think it was necessary to tell him, I had no intention of taking my own life—sleep was one thing, and the pills I took were my vehicle to an escape, but suicide was not an option. I believed from my religious teachings in all my childhood years in Sunday school that one doesn't get into heaven by committing suicide, and I had no plans of seeing myself to hell.

* * * *

Unbeknownst to me, Jeffery, Michelle and Mike had met with Dr. Jantz in order to discuss how they could help me. The overdose had scared them and they wanted to ensure it wouldn't happen again. Two times in less than a week they felt they'd almost lost their mother. Chesnutt's actions to his victims had spilled over into their friends and families.

Jeffery later told me that if the phone rang in the middle of the night he would become filled with fear that something bad had happened. Michelle armed herself with a gun and two Rottweilers, one trained to attack by a given word. We had all been victimized. We had all been changed by the actions of one.

Jeffery, Michelle and Mike arrived back at Mike's place. They had brought lunch for everyone and after brief introductions to Detective Bruce, they made their way to the kitchen to set up a buffet.

Detective Bruce commented on what nice kids I had and I assured him I wouldn't have gotten through the last several days without them. He pulled me to the couch, and we sat down. He put his arm around me and pulled me to his chest, "I think you need to let yourself cry," he said.

I slowly pulled away and said, "I don't want to.

"You're safe now, you're with people who care about you and love you, you can let yourself cry."

I chose not to. Looking back now, I understand that if I had cried, I would have been admitting that something more horrible than most people could comprehend had happened to me. It was a survival mechanism to shut down, to squelch emotion, to keep it all at bay.

* * * *

Cindy called and the plans were set for a weekend at a bed and breakfast at Long Beach, Washington, right on the ocean. She promised to handle all the details, all I had to do was be ready when she picked me up. It started to sound like something I could look forward to.

Michelle helped me pack and took care of gathering everything I would need for the weekend. I still wasn't thinking clear enough to accomplish even the smallest of tasks. Michelle and Jeffery seemed to know this instinctively and would just step in and take over, thank God.

I'm sure they wondered where their once secure, confident, independent mother had gone. As I watched her place my toothbrush, antibiotics and an extra sweater in the suitcase, it occurred to me how simple life had been before the attack, how naïve I'd been in my secure little world.

We arrived at the bed and breakfast just after dark, the door was locked and we had to ring the bell, I liked the fact that they kept the door locked. The friendly Norwegian owners greeted us and let us in, locking the door behind us.

They gave us a tour and told us the particulars about when breakfast would be served in the main dining room. We retired to our room and Cindy called Scott to let him know we had arrived safely. She positively bubbled when she talked to him, it was obvious they were in love.

I called Michelle and Jeffery and then we got ready for bed. I took an over the counter sleep aid that wasn't nearly as strong or as effective as the prescription I had been given, but it was better than lying awake all night. Cindy and I chatted for a while and then she asked if I thought I could fall asleep, "I think so," I said, knowing full well that sleep would be fleeting for at least a few more hours. She insisted I wake her if I needed anything.

It wasn't long before Cindy's breathing became deep and rhythmic. I missed the ease of which I used to fall asleep before the attack. I didn't want to wake her, she was sleeping like a "normal" person and I didn't want to rob her of that.

I focused on my children and Lily and how fortunate I was to have such a loving family. I thought about the many cards and flowers I'd received from caring local businesses and customers of the café. The handwritten notes from friends I'd left behind after my divorce from Tom, while I was forever grateful for the outpouring of kindness, I was oddly uncomfortable. I didn't feel deserving of all the compassion, nor did I understand the media blitz.

My mother had told me, "People get raped every day. You need to put this behind you and move on with your life. That's exactly what I wanted to do, I wanted my old life back, the one I knew and probably took for granted.

Sometime after 2am, while immersed in thoughts of the past and questions about the future, I fell asleep.

* * * *

I woke at 6am and laid in bed quietly until Cindy turned over and opened her eyes around 7:30am, "How did you sleep?" she asked. I told her I had slept fine, and we decided to get dressed and head to the dining room.

Breakfast was wonderful, a variety of homemade muffins, fresh fruit and perfectly prepared eggs. Our fellow visitors were friendly and cheerful and the atmosphere was warm and welcoming.

Even on little sleep, I was excited about the day that stretched before us; no real plans, we might go in search of a good coffee shop, a walk on the beach or to the local shops.

We would do all those things, including a little boutique gift shop where I bought Mike an Italian cookbook. He had been so kind in letting my family turn his home into Grand Central, he was a good friend and the book would be my way of saying thank you.

We walked the boardwalk and I felt the sun warm on my back and breathed the fresh sea air deep into my lungs. The brief escape from reality was proving good for me, it felt good, and I realized I felt the peace that the atmosphere brought—I felt something.

We sat on a bench and watched the thunderous waves roll in and crash along the beach. I closed my eyes and envisioned each wave advancing and receding back into the ocean, taking with it some of my pain. Each wave there for a purpose, to wash away the last week, Allan Chesnutt and all the havoc he wrecked on my life. The invasion that took place and the ruin that was left in its wake— each wave bringing with it a little ocean magic that would somehow heal me and send me on my way to a full recovery.

It sounded so easy, and yet, I knew that I should simply sit and listen to the sounds of the ocean, and gather strength for what was to come.

CHAPTER 13 – THE COMMUNITY GATHERS

"We would like to live as we once lived, but history will not permit it."
~*John F. Kennedy*

Monday morning came and I woke crying, no recollection of a dream, in fact—I had no thoughts what-so-ever. I stood next to the bed until the uneasiness passed, I found that my go-to for coping was to change my position or find a distraction when I became uncomfortable and eventually I'd calm down. It seemed to be my new way of surviving.

I had a nine-o'clock appointment with Dr. Jantz and then Jeffery took me to the courthouse in Everett to meet with the prosecutor, Dave Kurtz, and his assistant. They were a kind and gentle pair and began our meeting by inquiring as to how I was doing. I told them that without my children and my counselor, I didn't know how I could have possibly gone on.

They asked me to tell them in my own words what happened the night of the rape. I had excellent recall and was able to relay every detail. It was strange, I couldn't seem to make a decision about my business or even get dressed without help, but I could communicate every particular about the dreaded night. Dr. Jantz told me it was a classic case of post-traumatic stress and shock, I had no reason not to believe him; everything he had told me thus far had proven correct.

When I finished my testimonial of the ordeal, Dave spoke up, "I don't want to charge him with attempted murder, he'll most likely enter a plea of not guilty and this case will go to trial."

I felt betrayed, "He's getting off easy," I insisted.

"I understand your frustration," Dave said, "believe me, I'm as frustrated with the laws and loopholes as you are, but Chesnutt hadn't tried to kill the other victims, so it's going to be difficult to convince a jury that he tried to kill you."

I knew he meant well, I also knew that the laws were on the side of the guilty and the victims often are victimized, yet again. I'd seen my fair share of injustice when I was with Pierce County Rape Relief.

I left the meeting down and deflated.

* * * *

The next day I had an appointment with Liliana Fitzpatrick, my hairdresser. When she saw me she welled and hugged me tight, "God's watching you, Madeline, I'm so grateful He saved you from this horrible incident."

She told me she was thankful I was alive, I told her I wasn't so sure, "I feel like the walking dead." It was true, I was a zombie—a freak—a shell of my former self with no sense of direction, nothing to look forward to and no will to engage.

Today would be the first time I had driven my car since the attack. I wore a pair of mirrored sunglasses that I kept in the glove box on the chance a passenger might need a pair, I never wore them—until now. They hid my eyes completely, I called them my "I've just been raped," sunglasses.

I was hopeful that Liliana would somehow transform the woman I saw in the mirror, I wanted to see someone new, someone who had not been viciously attacked. But no amount of cut and curl could erase the fact that I had been changed on the inside, and those scars were not going anywhere fast.

I thanked Liliana for the beautiful flower arrangement she had sent and headed back to Mike's. That evening I was to meet my friends Molly and Megan, a couple of gals that worked at Robin Hood Lanes Bowling Alley, I'd often have coffee with them after my morning shift at the café. They had been wanting to see me and Jeffery drove me to meet them and then excused himself to take care of a few things for the business, he would meet us at Provinces restaurant in Edmonds when he was done.

Molly and Megan suggested we have a drink in the lounge while we waited for Jeffery. There were several people in the lounge and some were talking about, "the lady who captured the serial rapist," before I could protest, Molly spoke up and announced it was me they were talking about. Several approached our table to shake my hand and tell me I was a hero. They wished that I had, "killed the bastard." I began to cry, the attention made me uncomfortable. The people seemed taken aback at my response, they didn't understand it any more than I did.

When Jeffery arrived, I was shaking and told him what had happened. He suggested we move to the dining area and order dinner. I regained my composure and the dinner was marvelous, when we were through, I bid Molly and Megan goodbye and Jeffery drove me back to Mike's place.

Mike had a weekly game of Whirley Ball and was still not home when we arrived. Jeffery knew I was afraid of the dark and didn't want to leave me alone, but I could see that he was exhausted and I insisted I would be fine until Mike returned. At last I convinced him to go home and get some sleep, "Lily's waiting," I said.

Once Jeffery had left, it only took a few moments for me to lose my sense of being secure. I was not okay, the dark scared me and I didn't want to be there alone. I phoned my friend Kim and she suggested I come to her place. She had a roommate, but she said it wouldn't be a problem. I declined, thanking her, "Just stay on the phone with me," I asked.

We talked for a while and I began to calm down. Before we hung up, she reiterated her offer to have me stay with them and said to be sure and call again if I became the least bit panicked. I thanked her and we hung up.

I waited for Mike, pacing the kitchen and family room—back and forth, back and forth, again and again. He finally arrived home at 11:30pm, much later than usual and I was on him the minute he walked in, "I would have appreciated if you had let me know you were going to be so late!" I blurted.

I couldn't tell him I was scared, my new weakness embarrassed me. I felt I had no control over my life. Mike yelled back, "You know, I did have a life before this happened to you! You're pretty selfish to expect me to drop everything!"

I was stunned, I started to cry and left the room. I called Kim back and asked if I could take her up on the offer to stay with her and her roommate, "Should I come and get you?" she asked.

"No, I'll drive," I said. "I need my car."

I threw my clothes into a bag and began packing my car. It still hurt to pick up weight, but I did it anyway.

When I was done, I went and found Mike in the family room sitting on the couch. I was still crying as I told him I was going to Kim's. I told him I was sorry for the inconvenience and thanked him for letting me stay as long as he had.

"C'mon, Maddie. Don't do this," he motioned for me to sit on the couch next to him.

"No, I can't," I said, "I'm going to go." I started for the front door when he jumped up and said, "Don't go! You don't have to go! Just stay here."

I moved for the door, determined now more than ever to take my leave while I still had a shred of dignity, I had never been a burden in anyone's life and I didn't plan to start now.

"No!" I said as I opened the door, "Fine!" Mike yelled as he slammed the door behind me.

That would be my last moment in Mike's home for several weeks.

* * * *

Within an hour I was on Kim's couch, I refused her offer to sleep in her bed. I didn't want to disrupt her sleep and I knew how fleeting sleep could be for me at times, especially now, without my prescriptions.

I tossed and turned, I couldn't get comfortable and while there was only one entrance to the third floor apartment, I didn't feel secure. Kim's roommate, Renee wasn't home, Kim said she often slept at her boyfriend's house. At 6:30am I heard a key in the front door and Renee opened the door, she was surprised to see me on the couch.

Renee was a stylish girl with a perfect manicure and a great tan. Her hair was cropped just below her ears and it was a shade darker than Kim's red mane.

"I'm Madeline," I said. "I'm sorry if I startled you." She was kind and said, "I'm sorry I woke you." I told her I was already awake and she moved to the kitchen to make a pot of coffee. She offered me a cup and Kim came into the living room, "How did you sleep?" she asked.

"Fine," I lied. Kim asked Renee if she would join her in the other room for a moment. I knew I was going to be the topic of conversation and was feeling a little awkward. I was displaced, my home was no longer my home, Mike had alienated me out of his and I knew I couldn't leave Edmonds to stay with Jeffery or Michelle. I suddenly felt terribly alone.

They returned to the living room and said I could stay as long as I wanted to. I was grateful for their hospitality on such short notice. I called Jeffery and told him I'd be staying with Kim for a while, he didn't ask why and I didn't offer an explanation. I didn't feel the need to worry him with any more details, he had enough of a load to carry.

"How much longer can you run the café?" I asked.

"My boss is giving me six to eight weeks if needed," he said. His boss had shared that a close relative had been raped years earlier and he knew the impact it could have on the entire family, he asked about my progress every time he and Jeffery spoke.

The following day I had another appointment with Dr. Jantz, he asked me how things were going and I told him I had left Mike's and was staying with a friend. He agreed it was a good idea and that the most important thing was that I felt safe.

Then he asked how I was feeling, "I don't know," I said. It had become my pat answer.

"I want you to see another counselor," he said. "His name is Ian and I've made you an appointment for next Tuesday. I think you'll like him."

* * * *

I bounced around for the next several days; a weekend with Barbara and Bill, a couple of nights with Jeffery and Lily, and then back to Kim and Renee's. Tuesday arrived and I asked Kim if she'd accompany me to my appointment with Ian, it turned out that Ian was her counselor. Kim had been molested by her stepfather for years and had been seeing Ian regularly for the past five years in an effort to come to terms with not only the abuse, but the fact that her mother remained married to him.

I asked Ian if Kim could sit in on the session and he said that would be fine. We entered his office and sat down. He seemed nice, but I had grown accustomed to Dr. Jantz. I tried to maintain an open mind and did as I was asked.

He requested that I close my eyes and recount in detail the night of the attack. He placed a Kleenex box next to me and I shut my eyes and relayed the same story that I had told the prosecutor, the police and Dr. Jantz. It was becoming an all to familiar tale and I was finding the constant recanting a little annoying.

I could hear Kim attempting to stifle sobs and blowing her nose as I spoke, I was confused as to why she was crying and guessed it was because up until now, I hadn't shared the details of the attack with her. Perhaps I had become immune to the effects of the graphic nature of my descriptions.

When I was finished I asked, "Can I open my eyes now?"

"Yes," came Ian's reply. When I opened my eyes his expression was one of confusion, as if he couldn't figure me out.

"Have you let yourself cry over what happened to you," he asked.

"Why?" I responded, "What is there to cry about?" I suddenly wanted to leave.

We didn't quite get through the hour, I was anxious to get out of Ian's office, something about it made me claustrophobic and it felt odd that he would be so insistent that I cry on my first session with him. Crying, I felt, was a very personal thing, an outpouring of emotion that can only take place in a trusted environment. I wasn't feeling that there—not yet.

When Kim and I left, she told me how incredibly sad she felt when she heard the details of the attack. She'd had no idea what I had gone through. I insisted it didn't bother me and told her not to be upset.

She hesitated before speaking, "I don't think you're dealing with what happened," she said.

I had no response to offer, I felt she was entitled to her opinion...even if it was wrong.

CHAPTER 14 – LINE-UP

"You may have to fight a battle more than once to win it."
~Margaret Thatcher

Chesnutt was scheduled to be in a line-up the following day and the other victims were asked to identify him. I was told I didn't have to be present due to the fact they had collected plenty of DNA from the townhouse and me. I insisted on going, I wanted to know what he looked like. Dr. Jantz told me that even though I currently had no recollection of Chesnutt's face, my mind would know him when I saw him and I'd be able to pick him out of a line-up.

I was confident I would remember him, because when I took off the blindfold, his face must have etched itself somewhere in my mind, especially considering I held him at gunpoint. I felt it would be easy, if nothing else, his bandaged fingers would give him away.

Jeffery and Michelle drove me to the police station where the line-up was to take place. The other victims were in the waiting area and we were instructed not to speak to one another and they would take us one at a time to the viewing area. No one was to accompany us except Detectives Bruce and Jones and a representative from Chesnutt's attorney's office.

I asked if I could be the first one in, I was anxious to remember, feeling that perhaps if I saw him in captivity, I would find some peace. We were told that once we finished our viewing, we were to go to another area to fill out a form and leave without seeing the other victims again.

I was escorted into a tiny room where a single folding chair faced a closed curtain. The two detectives and Chesnutt's representative were crowded in the room with me.

"Once the curtain is opened, there will be a sheet of one-way glass. You are safe, they can't see or hear you," said Detective Bruce. They put a box of Kleenex next to me and closed the door.

"There will be ten men, one at a time they will approach the glass and turn to the left, right, and then face away from you," said Detective Jones, "can you give us a sentence he spoke the night of the attack? Each man will be instructed to repeat it.

Remember a sentence? Of course I could remember a sentence. The words had been playing over and over in my head since the attack, "Shut up," I said, "we're going to kill you."

Hearing myself say those words felt foreign to me, my mind had always been free of violence, and here—now, I was to concentrate on a sentence that was nothing but violent and I was to hear it at least ten more times in the next several minutes.

I was informed that once the ten suspects approach and say the line, I could have any one of them come back for a second look if need be. They asked if I was ready, I squared my shoulders, took a deep breath and said, "Yes."

The curtain was drawn open; the men were lined up, seated against the wall with their right hand hidden behind their back. They wore identical prison garb and stared expressionless. I scanned each face—I didn't recognize him. I began to feel hot and nauseous when my eyes trailed back to numbers 3 and 5, I was certain it was one of those two men.

"Number one, step forward," Detective Bruce's tone went from his usual gentle way with me to that of a stern commander. Number one stood and took a few steps toward me, "Turn to the right," said Detective Bruce. The convict complied.

"Turn to the left," he again did as he was told. I was shocked when he turned his back to me and his right hand was tucked in his jail pants. They weren't dumb, they knew I'd be looking for the injured fingers I had given my attacker. Now I would really have to concentrate.

Detective Bruce instructed him to step to a line a few inches from the glass. He was so close I felt I could have reached out and touched him.

"Repeat after me; Shut up! We're going to kill you!" A shiver went up my spine, hearing it in my head was one thing, but hearing it once again in a male voice was a little frightening.

"Shut up. We're going to kill you," Number one's delivery was dry and monotone.

"Go back to your seat," instructed Detective Bruce.

"Number two, step forward." The process continued until each man had stepped up and spoken the dreaded words. I asked only that numbers 3 and 5 repeat the process and then I had seen and heard enough.

I was escorted to another room and asked to fill out a form revealing my pick of Allen Ray Chesnutt from the line-up, I wrote that it was number five and if I was wrong, my second choice was number 3. I signed the form and Jeffery, Michelle and I were directed to a door, which led outside.

"It was either five or three," I said, "I'm positive."

The following day I called Detective Jones and asked if I had been correct in my pick.

"I'm afraid not, but don't worry, it was dark that night and we do have the evidence."

I was dumbfounded, how could my mind reject the image and voice of the man who changed the course of my life?

I tried to remember the faces of the remaining eight men, "Can you tell me which one he was?" I asked, I was desperate to know.

"I'm sorry, Madeline, I can't at this time."

I told him I understood and hung up.

The next day I had an appointment with Dr. Jantz and told him about the line-up and that I had gotten it wrong. "Your mind will only allow you to have as much information as you can handle," he said.

"Have you considered going back to work?" I knew the question would come up eventually and I didn't feel ready.

"Jeffery's doing a great job and, quite frankly, I don't want to be seen. What will the customers who know about it say to me?" I was being honest and I wasn't interested in being lauded a hero. I just wanted it all to go away, I could only imagine being the local draw; people would come for miles to be served a cup of brew by the lady who snagged her rapist.

"I want you to spend a night in the townhouse."

Was he crazy? "No!" I protested, "I can't do that."

He persisted, "You don't have to stay there alone," he said, "take a friend or one of your children, but you should overcome that hurdle if you want to go back to a normal life."

I told him I would think about it.

That evening Michelle called and asked if her boyfriend, Gabe, could stay at the townhouse. He had been commuting from Lake Tapps to Snohomish to work on a construction project. By staying at the townhouse, he could cut down on the long drives during the week. I told her he could, as I had no intention of staying there, "Dr. Jantz wants me to spend a night there, but I'm just not ready. To be honest, I don't know if I ever will be."

She saw Gabe's presence as an opportunity, "You'd be safe, Mom. You wouldn't be alone." I told her he was welcome to use the townhome until the construction job was over, but that was all I was offering.

Later Cindy called and we discussed the idea, "Why don't we have a slumber party?" she offered. "Scott can bring a sleeping bag and I can sleep with you in the bed." I reluctantly accepted her offer and we decided on the following night. We would have dinner together and then go directly to the townhouse.

* * * *

The following day I had an appointment with the tanning salon I had been frequenting before the attack. I walked in and Cyndi, the owner, greeted me in her usual friendly manner.

"Where have you been," she asked. "It's been a while since we've seen you."

I asked if she had heard about the capture of the Lynnwood/Edmonds serial rapist.

"Of course," she said, "everyone's talking about it. You know, he was going into two area salons and instead of tanning, he would climb the wall and watch the women tan naked. He was chased several times, but I guess he was really fast. I'm so glad they finally caught him."

"I'm the one who caught him," I said. Her mouth dropped open, "You? You're the one who had the gun?" I affirmed her question with a nod.

She got up from her desk and hugged me, "Oh my God, what a hero you are!" There was that word again; I assured her that anyone would have done what I did when confronted by that monster.

"Yes, but think about all those women you saved from him. I know the community is grateful."

I thanked her for her kind words and changed the subject by making another appointment.

Note: The next time I visited the salon, Cyndi presented me with a large, beautiful card that had been signed by lots of people I had never even met. She told me they had all chipped in and bought me a year's worth of tanning sessions. I started to cry, "They don't even know me," I said.

"It's their way of thanking you," she smiled as she handed me a tissue. I still couldn't fathom a group of strangers bringing forth such a kind and compassionate gesture on my behalf.

"Please thank every single person for me," I said. Cyndi promised she would.

The rest of the day flew by and soon it was time for me to meet Cindy and Scott for dinner. I was invited to their home and it was quite beautiful, it had a view of the water and they were in the process of remodeling, from the plans that Scott showed me, it would be even lovelier. Cindy prepared a wonderful dinner and then it was time to pack up and head for the townhouse.

I didn't like being there; it didn't feel like my home anymore. It had a somewhat stale odor of cleaning supplies and the air was stagnant, I would have liked to open the windows and let it circulate, but it was getting late and I wasn't about to risk leaving a window open.

We washed up for bed and Scott laid out his sleeping bag at the foot of my bed, Puka was close-by in her usual spot. I wondered if the room conjured up memories for her, too. Did she recall the violent blows to my face and body? The screams? The gunshots? I wished she could talk and tell me why she couldn't even muster a bark in protest. I now knew that fear was a strange thing for people, and now it seemed that it was a strange thing for animals as well.

I lay in bed and listened as Cindy and Scott's breathing became deep and rhythmic. I looked up to the window and thought, If only I hadn't been wearing earplugs. I might have heard him cut the screen. I could have gotten my gun before he ever got inside. I could have called 911 sooner.

My mind was cluttered with, *if onlys*. Somehow I managed to fall asleep and I was relieved when morning came quickly. We dressed and I thanked Cindy and Scott for staying with me. I didn't mention that I had no immediate plans to return permanently.

It just wasn't home any longer.

The love of my life, Tom Morehouse

Officer L.P. Miller, Edmonds Police Department and first on the scene.

Detective Jeff Jones, Edmonds Police Department

Detective Joe Bruce, Lynnwood Police Department

Dr. Gregory Jantz, my counselor, Edmonds Washington

Receiving medal at the Medal Of Valor Ceremony with Major General Barlow and Snohomish County Sheriff James Scharf (speaking) - 1994

Me and daughter Michelle Morehouse with Montel Williams –
1996

Son, Jeffery Morehouse

Me with Maury Povich - 1998

Lynnwood/Edmonds Serial Rapist Allan Ray Chesnutt

Code 10-71 Victim to Victor A True Story

CHAPTER 15 – THE ARRAIGNMENT

"Ladies and gentlemen, it's time to meet the Devil!"
~R.B. Harker

With Saturday's paper came the news that Chesnutt was scheduled to be arraigned that following Monday. He was being held in the Snohomish County Jail and if convicted of all ten charges, his sentence would range between 58 and 76 years in prison.

He had used a BB gun in at least four of the attacks and used a knife as his weapon of choice on the rest of his victims—me included. In his very first attack, he allegedly told the victim, "It's not your fault, it's mine. I'm the evil one."

During the attack Chesnutt was apparently quite talkative, inquiring about his victim's work and family. He also became agitated during the ordeal and had threatened to kill her.

"I grabbed her by the neck," he admitted to police, "I always put the knife on them somehow, just to let them know it's there. Then I raped her." His matter-of-fact manner as he spoke of his victims as less than human, made me feel sick.

It was also mentioned that the charges would include attempted robbery, as he tried to steal money from me to buy drugs. The charges were racking up nicely and it appeared that Chesnutt would be spending a long, long time in prison.

The following day I met Gabe at the townhouse and gave him the key, "Use it as long as you like," I said.

"Michelle said you might stay a night or two while I'm here," he was gentle in his delivery, and I knew he meant well, but I wasn't ready to commit.

"Maybe, we'll see," I said.

There was something different about the place, my once bright and cheerful home had been altered. It was tainted with fear, brutality and darkness. It wasn't like a trip to Bed Bath and Beyond for a few new throw pillows and a trendy lamp was going to mask what had happened there.

My desire to be there had been squelched and I didn't know how to get it back, or even if I wanted it back, something was nagging at me to cut my losses and leave the place behind. I decided to give myself a little more time. For now, I had the couch at Kim and Renee's place, and that would have to be my safe haven...for now.

* * * *

Monday arrived and I woke with the now familiar pit in my stomach, it was still not clear if Chesnutt would enter a plea of guilty or not guilty and the latter would definitely affect the next several months of my life. My plan was to be at the courthouse flanked by Jeffery, Michelle and a handful of friends and family who wanted to be by my side. I wanted my parents to go as well, I felt like a child who needed their nurturing.

I called my mother and was as straight as I could possibly be, "I'd like you to be there," I said. I didn't expect anything other than an assurance that they would, indeed, be there to support me; sadly, I was mistaken.

"Let me speak with your father and let you know," she said.

"What's to discuss?" I asked. I knew if my own children had been through something similar, an army couldn't keep me from being by their side.

"Someone might recognize us," she admitted. "A friend who doesn't know it's you might see us."

I was dumbfounded, "I have to go," I said. I needed to hang up before I began to cry. They're embarrassed! I thought. To make matters worse, my sister refused to accompany me as well, she had "too many things to do."

I was confused, the community was hailing me a hero and members of my own family refused to show support. It was clearly a time to look to new-found friends as my much-needed support system. Aside from my children and my former in-laws, my immediate family was not on board with seeing me through the reality of a rape.

I suddenly longed for simpler times, the days on the lake before Tom's affair, before the divorce that put me on the path of a single mom and working girl. I closed my eyes and pictured the sun glistening off the water in early June. I heard the speedboats and the laughter of skiers as they recovered from a spill into the drink.

For just a moment, I was there. For just a moment, I was at peace. Then I opened my eyes.

* * * *

The courtroom was packed. Detective Bruce found seats for Michelle and I and sat down next to me, "Is he here?" I asked.

Detective Bruce nodded, "Yes, he's the one standing up front in the orange uniform," he said. "He's got shackles on his legs."

I strained to look, but there were so many people in the courtroom that I couldn't get a good look. It felt odd and a little morbid to me, why did I want to see him? What was I searching for in getting a glimpse of his face? Closure? Assurance that they had the right man?

It felt like a car accident on the freeway, you pass, all the while straining to see the carnage; the moment that lives were changed—maybe a little, and maybe a lot. But rest assured, lives were changed.

Judge Joseph A. Thibodeau read the charges and asked Chesnutt if he understood each one, he responded with, "Yes."

"How do you plead," asked the judge.

"Guilty." That was all we needed to hear.

The people in the courtroom gasped, a man called out, "Loser!" Another followed with, "You're going to make a pretty girl in prison."

I was taken aback when Michelle yelled, "You're going to die!"

"Michelle!" I said, I turned to her as she rose and ran from the courtroom.

Judge Thibodeau pounded his gavel, "Order in the courtroom," he demanded. "Any more outbursts and I will clear this courtroom!"

It was announced that sentencing would be set sometime in July and the court was adjourned.

It was over.

* * * *

Jeffery found Michelle and they met me in the prosecutor's office. Myself and a few of the other victims had congregated there to regain our composure after the trauma of seeing Chesnutt again. Michelle was upset, but no longer in tears. The press had set up satellite dishes and Detective Jones told me he'd take us down another way to avoid the cameras.

We started down the stairs to the first floor when he stopped, "Take my arm," he said. I looked at him and could see his stare fixed on the bottom of the stairs, there was an older gentleman standing next to a cameraman. I took hold of Detective Jones' arm and braved the descent.

"Are you ever going to give us an interview?" the man asked. I ignored him and heard Kim say, "Why don't you leave her alone?" I was later told it was John Sanderford from King 5 News. He most likely recognized Jeffery and Michelle from recent interviews and surmised who I was. Once safely beyond the pair, I thanked Detective Jones for helping us out.

As we walked across the courtyard we were forced to pass another news crew. "The cameras are off," the reporter said, "I just want to tell you how sorry I am about what happened to you and—well, I was hoping you'd give us a short interview."

I appreciated his compassionate approach and decided it was inevitable that I would eventually give in and grant an interview, it might as well be sooner than later. He assured me they would stop any time I asked.

"Are you ready?" he asked.

"Yes," I said.

He led in by saying that Chesnutt's last victim had just left the courtroom, then turned to me, "I know this has been difficult for you. How do you feel about the guilty plea?"

I felt my face flush and my eyes well, "It doesn't change anything," I managed. "It's really been hard." Michelle put her arms around me and we both began to cry.

The reporter went on to say that many were pulling for me. He signed off and then turned to me, "Thank you. We won't be using your name." I nodded in appreciation and we headed to the car.

That evening Jeffery, Michelle, Lily and I went to the townhouse to catch the 5:00 news. The arraignment was the top story, when I saw myself on TV I only had one thought, I have a dress like that. It felt like I was watching someone else—someone who looked like me, even dressed like me, but that person was not me.

I could vaguely hear the kids commenting on the reporter's sensitivity and that they thought the interview went well. They flipped channels and the story led every local station. I couldn't understand what the big deal was, I didn't feel it was all that newsworthy.

* * * *

Over the next several days the local news continued to touch on Chesnutt's capture. Jim Forman of KOMO-TV did a special report on how local women were arming themselves, "following the example of the Edmonds woman who captured the Lynnwood/Edmonds serial rapist."

He was reporting from the Continental Sportsman and showed B-roll of women taking firing lessons. The ironic thing was that Michelle, Gabe and I were there one afternoon when they were interviewing a few of the women and taking video. Michelle had also purchased a gun and was learning to become comfortable with it. We took aim at paper targets, pretending they were Chesnutt, we were thrilled at the perfect holes we made in his head and chest.

Forman studied us, but I don't think he recognized me. If so, he surely would have hounded me for an interview.

Michelle and Gabe had been urging me to stay at the townhouse overnight since Gabe was there most nights. I was reluctant, but I decided to try again.

CHAPTER 16 – SENTENCING

"Justice will be served."
~John Eklund

The following week I bounced between Kim's couch and the townhouse, but only on the nights that Kim was able to stay there with me. Then Mike started calling me again and after several dinner dates, I began sleeping at his house again. My days were filled with counseling appointments, tanning sessions and lunches and dinners with friends. It seemed the busier I kept, the more I could convince myself that, just maybe, life could return to normal.

On June 15th, a mere month and two days since the attack, I received a letter from the prosecuting attorney's office stating that Chesnutt would be sentenced on Friday, July 23, at 1pm before The Honorable Judge Thibodeau.

The letter contained an invitation to attend the sentencing and stated that if I'd like an opportunity to speak at the sentencing, I should advise prior to the day of. It also stated that I could write the judge a letter to let him know my feelings about the sentence. It went on to say where I should mail it and gave a number to call should I have any questions—it was signed by, David A. Kurtz, Deputy Prosecuting Attorney.

I called Kurtz's office to ask what they meant about speaking at the sentencing,

"It's your chance to verbally confront Allan Chesnutt in the courtroom," she said.

I instantly panicked, "No! I don't want to get up in front of him. I want to be there, but I don't want him to see me!" Kurtz's assistant told me that some of the other victims and their family members were going to address Chesnutt directly, but she understood that I wasn't comfortable in doing so since my attack had been so recent.

"Remember that your close family members can speak if they desire, and they, as well as friends, can write letters too," I felt that she really wanted to ensure we took advantage of the opportunity to have our say in court.

Just the thought of sitting down and drafting a letter that would convey what Chesnutt had done to me was exhausting. I was constantly on alert while trying to dodge bouts of depression and hopelessness. I was so fearful it could happen again, someone would crawl in a window, follow me in a parking lot, or leap out of a dark alleyway. A single fantasy replayed over and over in my mind; me with a gun pointed directly at Chesnutt's head as he lay face down on the floor—a single shot to the head and this time, I kill him.

I'd made an appointment with my general practitioner and told him how I was feeling. He suggested Prozac for the depression, I didn't like the thought of an antidepressant, it made me feel weak and out of control, but I needed something and so I agreed to fill the prescription.

Once on it, the Prozac made me scatterbrained. I'd lock my keys in my car two or three times a week and call the police or AAA to unlock my car, they didn't mind, but I was embarrassed.

Jeffery was still getting calls from the media inquiring about my recovery and pressing for an interview. One in particular had discovered that I owned the café and threatened to release my name. Jeffery called the station and swore he would sue if they mentioned me during a single report.

Detective Jones called to tell us that CNN, along with several smaller networks, was demanding the 911 tape, they insisted it was public information. He assured us the 911 tape was safe with them and I wasn't to worry. He let on that some television shows were also in contact with them, looking for information on how to get in touch with me. He knew I wanted nothing to do with them and promised to continue to protect my retreat into seclusion.

But my time in hiding couldn't last forever. Jeffery was scheduled to head to Boston the week following the sentencing, and Dr. Jantz encouraged him to begin transitioning me back into the daily business practices. He felt the distraction and the return to something familiar would be healthy for me and might help me to find that sense of normalcy that I now lacked.

I composed my letter to the judge using the outline suggested to me by the prosecuting attorney's office:

Please describe in your own words, the physical, emotional or psychological impact this crime has had upon you and your family.

I began typing and the words spilled out—

Allan Chesnutt drastically affected my life. He told me fifteen to twenty times that he was going to kill me as he cut me with his knife, and I believe that he would have killed me. He tried to twist and break my neck. The effects on my life has been so great that I have trouble putting it into words.

I'm dealing with things I never had to deal with. I feel I am a different person, I am not happy, I suffer from depression and a general fear of people; especially men. Despite my attempts to overcome fear, I isolate more. I need to have trusted people stay with me and I have yet to spend a night alone.

I suffered a great deal of bodily trauma; including a broken toe, multiple cuts, trauma to my heart and nose from his stomping on my chest and face. I still suffer from an injured leg and I have difficulty breathing. I now suffer from insomnia, which was never a problem for me before.

I am self-employed and was physically unable to run my business for six weeks. I would have lost my business had I been unable to get someone to manage it for me.

I have always been an emotionally sound person and have never experienced a "flashback" before this happened. One week after the attack I was back in the emergency room, having had a terrifying flashback of the ordeal and accidentally overdosing on prescribed sleeping pills—anything to stop the horror that I was, again, experiencing.

I have great difficulty concentrating, particularly when it comes to business related tasks. I have a great deal of fatigue and an inability to relax. In addition to my own symptoms of depression, I recognize them in my daughter and my son suffers from total exhaustion.

I reread each sentence and realized the extent of damage those few hours had caused. They were powerful; having taken my once pretty calm and happy life and turning it into painful chaos that trickled down into my children's lives. The second question would pile onto the collateral damage:

Describe any financial impact the crime has had on you and/or your family.

Where was I to begin? The café, my son's career being put on hold, the uncertainty if I would be able to continue as a sole proprietor of my business, my counseling—that seemed only the tip of the iceberg. My answer seemed almost too short and simple.

Financially, the impact has been great for myself and my son and daughter. We lost wages and income, I had to spend a lot of extra money and have lost time away from my business. I've been in counseling to deal with the trauma and it will have to continue.

I had a storage unit built near my business since I cannot lift much weight due to the injuries on my chest and shoulders. It is difficult to put into quantifiable terms the amount this has cost me financially, but I assure you, it has been great.

Describe any permanent or long-lasting changes in your lifestyle, relationships or career resulting from the crime that may not have already been described...

The questions went on; how much damage was done? What would I like the judge to take into consideration when deciding the sentence?

I answered to the best of my ability—as did my parents when they wrote the judge.

We the parents of Madeline were, and are, devastated. As are all of our family by the impact of this crime, committed by serial rapist, A. Chesnutt.

They went on to say how the shock had caused them emotional distress, how they cried that their daughter had been put through such devastation. How it was time that rapists were given justifiable sentences that took them off the street and made the world safer for women everywhere.

They spoke of their health being affected by the ordeal that their daughter had endured. They cried out for the safety and wellbeing of women everywhere.

Their letter was eloquent and clearly said far more than they were able to convey to me. I had no idea they had been so greatly affected by my plight.

These are animals that should be caged for life, and we question whether their lives should be spared at all, when one considers the lasting effects on his many victims.

I was touched to find they were so stoically in my corner.

My sister wrote;
No one should ever have to go through this! The affect it has on me personally, as her sister, is to see what she is having to go through to deal with the whole ordeal. Had she not been so vigilant, I might not have a sister right now—

My ex-sister-in-law wrote;
The physical and emotional damage done by Mr. Chesnutt to his victims will affect them the rest of their lives. His actions have had a profound effect on each and every member of my family and made us victims as well. The male members are as outraged as the female members...

No one was untouched, even my nephew.

The Chesnutt's of the world make women look at all men as potential predators. He concluded a lengthy speech about the terror Allan Chesnutt brought to entire families by saying, Please give serious consideration to the maximum sentence possible for it would truly be in the best interest of the public's safety.

My niece spoke volumes for all of us when she said; Give the maximum sentence possible, and in the process, maybe bring a little peace to his victims, their families and those who could become his victims should he regain his freedom.

Her message was clear, "Don't let this animal do it again!"

Kim had asked if I'd give a friend of hers who worked as a popular local DJ on a radio show an interview. While I wanted to repay Kim for her kindness and grant an interview, I was afraid, I didn't trust myself to articulate what was on my mind. It always seemed to come out as gibberish. I asked if I could consider doing the interview at a later date.

My experience with the victims of sexual assault with the Pierce County Rape Relief told me that Chesnutt might very well not receive the appropriate sentence, given the seriousness of his crime. I felt that maybe it was time to speak up; let the public know how much damage he had done.

I decided to give an interview to Jolayne Houtz, a local reporter who seemed sensitive and unobtrusive. I had forgotten that I had promised the first interview to Darrell Glover should I ever decide to give one.

Two days before sentencing, the interview appeared on the front page of The Seattle Times.

Rapist's Captor Hailed as Hero: lives each day as victim.

The article offered nothing new to my story, it just detailed the attack, my overdose and my daily struggle to regain some sense of normal. It wasn't entirely accurate, but nevertheless, I thought it was well done.

When Darrell Glover saw the story, he contacted Jeffery and reminded him that he had been promised first crack at an interview. Jeffery called me and gently reiterated their conversation, "Mom, he was the one you promised the first interview to—if you ever gave one."

I felt terrible, it was less a betrayal and more an oversight on my part. I contacted Darrell and apologized profusely, he was most gracious and asked if I'd meet him for an interview. I agreed and we settled on a restaurant in Edmonds. I never let on to where I was staying at any given time, for fear the press would just show up and invade my privacy, as well as the privacy of those I was staying with.

The night before I was to meet with Darrell Glover, Mike and I went out for drinks. We started the evening with wine and oysters on the half shell. Jeffery had begun weaning me back on the business and so we picked up the bag of money from the last shift at the café and I shoved it under the seat in Mike's Porsche.

It was a warm summer night and for the first time in a long time, I was feeling good. The wine helped me relax and the food was good. We drank, joked and laughed; we were having a great time and decided to go to another restaurant for dinner. It was an Italian place and a favorite of both Mike's and mine.

We were seated and served drinks and as we waited to order, Mike made reference to all the media attention that had been given the case. I told him I wished it had never happened and had no interest in being a part of the media circus.

"You've been on the news more than anyone I've ever known," he said.

I was furious, I forgot there were other patrons in the restaurant and simply jumped up from the table, "If you're referring to the rape, you can go to hell!" I cried. "Do you think I wanted to be raped?"

He raised his voice at me, which made me even madder. I was unaware of the other patrons as I reacted to what I felt was a verbal attack. I marched to the car and retrieved the bag of receipts from the café, the manager followed me out and asked if everything was alright, "Call me a cab!" I demanded.

I had nowhere to go but the townhome and asked the cab driver to take me there. I was apprehensive about being there, but I had nowhere else to go. Once inside the townhouse, I had a message on my answering machine; it was Mike.

"If you think I was referring to your being raped, you need to get your head out of your ass. I would never have meant that."

I suddenly had no desire to return to his place, but I was afraid and not prepared to spend the night alone in the townhouse. I called Kim and asked if she'd spend the night with me. She agreed and I could hardly wait for her to get there.

The next day I met with Darrell Glover, he was as nice in person as he had been on the phone. The morning before the sentencing, his story appeared on the front page of the Seattle Post-Intelligencer:

Rapist-Stopper Pays No Mind to Heroism – with a subtitle that read, Gunfire halted assailant and kept him at bay for police.

The article was thorough, it touched on the importance of responsible gun ownership, the dangers of pulling a gun on one's attacker and the interview ended with my quote that, "had I known there was a final bullet in the gun, I would have used it to kill the man who blindfolded, raped, cut, kicked and beat me." Seeing those words in print made me understand the brutality of what had been done to me.

The article continued to touch on my thoughts with the flashback and the sleeping pills, as well as the ongoing trauma rape victims experience. A number of local newspapers ran with knock-offs of the same interview.

The articles mentioned my name, the cat was out of the bag and I was a local celebrity by default.

Something I had never asked for.

* * * *

I called my parents to ask if they would come to the sentencing since the prosecutor's office wanted names of anyone who would be attending. I was hurt when again, they said, "No."

"The kids are going to be with you, right?" my mother asked.

"Yes," I said, "but it would be nice if you could be there, too," I said.

After much coaching, they agreed to meet us at Caffé Paris for a quick lunch before following us to the courthouse. My mother was adamant that she didn't want to be seen with us walking into the courthouse, she in no way wished to be on television. I didn't understand her worry and wished they weren't so embarrassed to be with me and could sit with me in support during this difficult time, I had to simply take comfort in the fact that they were there.

Mike called me that evening to ask who would be accompanying me to the sentencing, neither he, nor I, mentioned our falling out in Seattle and he seemed pleased that my parents would be attending the sentencing. He asked me to call him when it was over and I promised I would.

The next day Michelle picked me up for lunch. We met Jeffery, Lily and my parents at a local restaurant. There wasn't a lot of time before the sentencing and my appetite was slim to none, so we ate quickly. Michelle commented that she planned to punch Chesnutt if she had the chance, I told her there would be plenty of security and it was probably best if she didn't try such a noble feat.

"I don't care," she said, "maybe I'll just spit on him as I walk by." I was grateful for her obvious support for me, but I made sure she considered her own safety.

"Whatever you do, be careful," I implored. Jeffery had planned to speak before the court as well, and I gave him a short statement thanking Detectives Bruce and Jones on my behalf.

My parents kept a safe distance behind us, they acted as if they didn't know us and we respected their wishes by doing the same. It stung a little, but I had already endured so much hurt, I actually felt numb to much more.

The courtroom was packed and people were straining to see what was going on inside. The media was there in force and Detective Jones appeared, as if by magic, and whisked me through the metal detector. I was so grateful; I didn't know if I could handle being manhandled by the press during this emotionally charged event. It was bad enough that I would have to be in the same room as Chesnutt, being briefed on my feelings about it seemed to just add insult to injury.

The fiancé of one of the victims gave me his seat, I was exactly four rows behind Chesnutt. His table was flanked by guards and his back was to me, but I was well aware of his proximity to me.

I looked around the courtroom and saw that my parents had been seated, I began to feel nervous and nauseated. A victim seated next to me took my hand and held it as we both waited for the judge to arrive.

There was an unspoken language among victims, a sisterhood that cannot be explained. We had never shared a conversation or a cup of coffee, but here we were kindred in an entirely different way. We knew what it was to be under his knife, his threats and demands. We shared something that only eight others in the room shared. We were unwilling members of a cult that had come to despise Allan Ray Chesnutt.

The judge entered the courtroom and we all stood, then sat again. I felt the fog take over, my eyes welled with tears that overflowed and streamed down my face. He may have been the one in shackles, but I was still the prisoner of that night.

One by one, Chesnutt's victims rose and approached the bench. They were shaking and many were crying. They told of how the events of their attack had ruined their lives. They spoke of not feeling safe anymore. They spoke of how they had to move and how they had to get counseling to deal with what Chesnutt had put them through.

I was stunned at their bravery, one actually demanded that Chesnutt look at her as she spoke. She was crying and shaking uncontrollably and couldn't read the statement she had prepared. She had to put it on a table in front of her, away from her shaking hands, to read it to the court. I looked over to where Chesnutt was sitting, he was slumped in his chair, obviously not all that pleased with what he was forced to hear.

I felt a hand on my shoulder and looked up to see Scott. He hadn't told me that he would be coming and I was both surprised and touched that he was there. He was in his work clothes, which told me he had sacrificed work to come and be there for me. It made me realize how many people supported me and that felt good.

Family members were allowed to speak and they were brave and brazen as they spoke of, "jumping over the table and killing you..." The guards went on high alert, but the message was clear—Chesnutt had few friends in that courtroom and many more who wouldn't have minded to see him dead.

One victim's brother appeared to scan the room, obviously considering whether the odds of scaling the table and strangling Chesnutt before the guards could get to him were in his favor. I hoped he wouldn't risk his own life for the animal who had already made victims of not only his sister, but of his entire family. I hoped he'd concentrate his efforts on supporting his sister to a full recovery, she needed his obvious love for her much more than any satisfaction an exercise in retaliation could bring her.

After many had stood to express their disdain for Chesnutt, Scott was called to speak. He was less angry than he was sad. He told Chesnutt that his actions had ruined lives, he wiped away tears as he told him that while he could not un-do what he had done, Scott hoped he'd, "...live the rest of his life the right way. The only thing to do now is to pray for God's forgiveness."

Michelle and Jeffery were the last to be called. Michelle barely made it past Chesnutt when she began to crumble. She started to cry and Jeffery was quickly by her side. She couldn't regain her composure to speak and handed her written statement to Jeffery.

I was oddly aware that my children were before me and my rapist. It felt surreal and I was desperately trying to stay in the moment. I wondered if Chesnutt's ego was soaring at the display of how his actions continued to affect his victims and their loved ones. If so, it was about to be squelched.

Michelle's hatred for Chesnutt remained visible, even through her tears. Jeffery finished his statement and cupped Michelle's elbow as they made their way back to their seat. I was grateful as they passed Chesnutt that Michelle didn't lunge at him. I was growing weary of this monster affecting our lives, I just wanted the ordeal to be over. I turned to see that my parents were still in the courtroom, my mother was crying. I turned back to face the judge and Chesnutt and the guard beside him stood up.

"Because of the violent, escalating nature of your acts, Mr. Chesnutt, if it were up to me, I'd sentence you to spend the rest of your life in prison. But, it's not up to me, I have to follow the law, and so, I sentence you to the maximum allowable time—seventy-seven years in prison without the possibility of parole."

There was a collective "gasp" of relief, reporters dashed from the courtroom and we all stood as Judge Thibodeau took his leave. Jeffery, Michelle and Lily made their way to me, "It's over," said Michelle.

I wanted to believe her, but I knew I was a long way from any sense of normal. The next hour was filled with a flurry of victims and their families hugging and recapping the verdict. The press was everywhere and Detective Jones offered me solace, "You can hide here," he offered.

As I disappeared into the safety of the prosecutor's office, I heard another victim shout, "Leave her alone! If you want an interview, I'll give you one!"

Jeffery, Lily, Michelle and my parents followed us into the prosecutor's office and after some private time and conciliatory hugs, I thanked my parents for coming and they told me they were glad they had.

Mike called to tell me he had heard about the sentencing. I told him the other victims and their families would be heading to Fishhouse Charlie's in Edmonds for dinner and dancing. I didn't feel much like celebrating, but I felt obligated to share in the collective relief that Allan Chesnutt would not be terrorizing the women of greater Seattle anytime soon. Mike and I left the restaurant, it had been a long day and I needed rest.

The next morning, Mike handed me the Post-Intelligencer, it had a picture of Chesnutt being escorted and the headline screamed, "Rapist, Reviled by Victims, Given 77 Years!" The article was thorough in its account of the sentencing, "You disrespected us, you raped us and tortured us with guns and knives, now it's your turn..." read a quote from one of his victims. "I promise we will forget you. We may not forget your vile actions, but we will forget you."

The article went on to describe Chesnutt's demeanor; his red eyes, his apology to his victims and his hope that, "God will forgive me."

The defense attorney was less optimistic, "He's going to die in prison. People don't live that long in prison. I hope this helps his victims. I hope they can get on with the rest of their lives."

What he failed to understand was that our lives had been altered forever. Nothing would ever be the same.

CHAPTER 17 – COMING APART

"Either you deal with what is the reality, or you can be sure that the reality is going to deal with you."

~Alex Haley

It was time to go back to work and my clients were glad to see me. Many brought up, in a gentle way, what had happened. They took my hands in theirs and looked at me with pained expressions, offering their apologies and praising me for what I had done.

It wasn't long before it became too much, I couldn't take the unwanted attention or the sympathy, I began to disassociate myself from the story in order to maintain my composure, "That wasn't me," I'd claim. "That was my twin sister." Their response would be one of confusion, but my unscrupulous efforts usually resulted in the subject being changed, and that's what I wanted.

We'd had a shed built next to the café to store milk. I could no longer lift the heavy crates in and out of the car, so trips to the local market were replaced with deliveries two days a week. With the purchase of two refrigerators, it was a costly endeavor, but now the employees could unlock the shed and cart the heavy crates inside.

I went for my second HIV test, it had been ten weeks since the attack, so this would be the test that would show any changes to my cells and indicate the presence of the virus. The results would be in the following week, I fantasized about somehow getting to Chesnutt and killing him if he had given me and the other victims this despicable death sentence. I felt that if it were the last thing I ever did—I would kill him.

The Edmonds and Lynnwood Police stations continued to be inundated with calls from local and national talk shows trying to reach me. I knew my privacy was being protected, but I also knew they were showing no signs of letting up and I found that troubling. I had no intention of going on any talk shows or giving any more live interviews, to do so would be to admit that it all really happened; that it was serious—and I was becoming very good at making a joke of it rather than dealing with it.

Dr. Jantz insisted my response was normal, "It's your way of coping," he said. "It's a survival technique."

He asked that I begin a journal and document my journey, "You have a story, Madeline. You can help other victims and their families."

I was skeptical that I could be of any help to anyone else, I couldn't even help myself. I suspected it was his way of forcing me to deal with my plight head on.

My best friend, Patti, had given me a journal the first time she had seen me after the attack, "Write your experience," she told me. "Spill it onto the page and get it out of your system."

I tried one night to do just that, but couldn't get past the part about waking up on the floor of my bedroom with Chesnutt's knee and a knife in my back. I tucked the journal away and never brought it out again.

* * * *

Jolayne Houtz from The Seattle Times sent me a letter through the Lynnwood Police Department, Detective Bruce brought it to me. In the letter, she thanked me for taking the time to speak to her the previous week and mentioned a reporter from "Inside Edition", a tabloid television show, was interested in doing a story on my case. She included his name and phone number and told me she'd leave it up to me as to whether I wanted to get in touch.

A producer from KIRO-TV also stopped by the station and left her card and a letter requesting my appearance on a talk show, "...that is produced by women, for women." The letter went on to say they would respect my voice and allow me to tell my story the way I wanted to, but they felt it was one their audience would want to hear. They had a call into my attorney to arrange a meeting—I advised the attorney that I wasn't interested.

My HIV test came back negative. I thought I would be thrilled at the news, but I had no feeling about it one way or the other. I was exhausted at the end of every day, but still had trouble sleeping.

One evening Mike and I had dinner with his son, after which we all went back to Mike's house. He went out to mow the lawn and suddenly I heard him yelling at the top of his lungs at his son. I went outside to attempt to calm him down and he turned his wrath on me.

The verbal attack was too much and I retreated back into the house. That night we didn't talk, I felt like a victim all over again and knew I couldn't allow myself to be around his temper any longer. The following morning, I gathered my belongings and went to the cafe.

That night I had dinner at a local pizza place with one of my employees. Her name was Lexus and she had a unique sense of humor. She had heard me tell customers that it was my twin who had caught Chesnutt and not me, she found it hilarious and before I knew it, we were howling as we concocted a fictitious story about how I lured a poor slob into my home at gunpoint and forced him to confess to raping me.

"I made him bite his own fingers to the bone," I could hardly get the words out, I was laughing so hard. "I took a knife and stabbed myself in the shoulder, then cut my arm and hand." Tears ran down our faces as I recalled, "kicking the wall until my toe broke."

Just then, Detective Jones entered the restaurant with his wife. He approached our table with a big smile and introduced me to her. I don't think he had ever seen me smile genuinely, much less, laugh; his expression made it clear he was happy to see me having fun for a change.

"I have a confession to make," I said, "you have the wrong guy. Chesnutt didn't do it." Detective Jones' smile quickly dissipated as I went on to convey the story Lexus and I had just made up. He knew I was kidding, but the uneasy look on his face spoke volumes; he was concerned for my emotional wellbeing.

"I'm just kidding," I said. I suddenly felt awkward that he didn't share in the hilarity that Lexus and I did. He politely excused himself with a promise to call me in the coming days and they went to be seated for dinner.

"I can't believe you told him that!" said Lexus.

"Nobody has a sense of humor anymore," I said. I tried to continue with the jokes about Chesnutt being innocent, but the moment was lost. The following week I told Dr. Jantz of my encounter with Detective Jones and briefly touched on the joke—Dr. Jantz didn't laugh either, he only jotted something on his tablet. I was beginning to feel my mental state was under a microscope and I was less than comfortable.

I decided it was stupid to continue to pay rent at the townhouse. I considered getting an apartment in the same complex as Kim and Renee, but there was no point in pretending that things were going to return to normal—I wasn't going back to the townhouse.

* * * *

Puka was fourteen years old. She was having trouble seeing and would walk into walls, on top of that, she had developed an odor that smelled like death. I made an appointment with the vet and Kim and Renee said they'd come with me. I knew I'd need moral support in the event that I had to put her down.

My worst fears were confirmed when the doctor told me that Puka had a heart condition that would only give her another three or four months to live. I knew what the humane thing to do was, her quality of life had declined and, as for me, I was scared to move into a new place with a dog who couldn't hear or bark to alert me to an intruder.

"She won't feel anything," the doctor promised. I began to cry and I kissed my longtime companion goodbye.

The doctor left to prepare the serum and Renee and I hugged as she had also begun to cry. The doctor returned and asked, "Are you sure you want to stay?"

"Yes," I insisted.

I stroked my sweet dog as the doctor began to inject her. She lay still as the serum began to take hold. Her eyes were open, but she couldn't move. The doctor put the stethoscope to her chest, "It's okay, Puka. You can go to sleep."

Minutes went by and she wasn't dying. I became more and more upset, suddenly wanting to take back my consent. I began sobbing, "Puka! I love you! Puka—oh, Puka."

The doctor looked to Renee, "Maybe you should take her to the other room." Renee gently coaxed me out of the room and Kim promised to stay with Puka until the end. Several minutes passed before the door opened and the doctor told me it was okay to come back in for one final "goodbye".

Puka's eyes were open and her still, lifeless body lay on the cold, hard table. The doctor said it took longer than usual due to her heart condition, her circulation was slow and it took a long time for the serum to reach her heart.

"She didn't suffer," she added. I kissed Puka goodbye one last time as Kim and Renee assured me I had done the right thing—I wasn't so sure.

In the last month, I had lost my sense of safety, my home, Mike and now my canine companion for the last fourteen years. My life as I'd known it had unraveled and I wasn't sure how much more I could take.

CHAPTER 18 – THE FIRST STEPS

"It was wearying, trying to adjust to all the paces life required."
~Larry McMurty

Both Jeffery and Michelle were covered under crime victim's compensation for counseling due to the severity of the crime and the personal impact on each of them. Up until this point, they had declined the service, but a scare at Michelle's home had her reconsidering.

She had returned one evening to a dark, empty house and was convinced the dog, a Rottweiler, was acting odd.

"...like someone's in here," she said. She was on the phone with me, curled up on the floor in her dining room clutching her gun, afraid to move.

"Leave!" I demanded, "Run to the neighbor's and call the police." I felt helpless, I wanted to protect her, even though she lived an hour away.

"Please, just stay on the phone with me," she begged.

"Your house was locked when you left, so no one should be in there." I stayed on the phone with her for the next twenty minutes until Gabe arrived and checked the house. No one was there.

"You and your brother must consider counseling," I said. My daughter had always been so brave, but here she was, realizing her vulnerability. She now understood that a vicious crime could happen to anyone, without warning.

Chesnutt still had so much control over us with the fear he had instilled. Now realizing the affect he had on my children, I felt my fear slowly being displaced by anger. Something in me was stirring, I was suddenly determined to get our lives back on track, and I'd start with a new apartment.

* * * *

I rented a unit just down from Kim and Renee's and was scheduled to take occupancy the first of September. I had continued to stay with them after Puka had died, I was considering getting another dog before I moved, I wanted the extra eyes and ears.

A client at the café often drove up with her Maltese, Rosebud, in her lap. She insisted that Rosebud didn't shed, because the breed has hair, rather than fur. I loved Rosebud, she was loyal with a sweet personality and I'd never seen a more affectionate dog.

I looked in the newspaper and found a breeder of Maltese puppies. I made an appointment and asked Michelle to accompany me, she had worked at a veterinary clinic and I felt I could use her expertise to determine if the pups were healthy and well-bred.

The puppies were only three weeks old and just tiny balls of white with jet black noses and dark eyes. There were three of them; two males and a female. The female was the tiniest; feisty and playful, she held her own with the larger pups and seemed to call all the shots. She'd nudge her way in to nurse, ensuring that she claimed her spot at the buffet that was their mother.

The breeder said she'd grow to no more than five pounds. Females cost more than males, due to their breeding capabilities, which didn't matter to me as I had no plans to breed her. I plunked down half of the $650 to hold her until I could bring her home in three weeks. I held her for a few moments longer and felt a surge of love travel through me.

Without a real plan in place, somehow a new lease on life was beginning to evolve.

* * * *

I arranged for a moving company to move me and Renee agreed to help me pack up the townhouse. Since my new apartment would be much smaller, I had secured a storage unit nearby to store the furniture and other items I wouldn't be taking to the apartment.

We were packing up the kitchen when Renee spotted blood on the refrigerator. Later, while cleaning the very bathroom I had held Chesnutt at gunpoint, I spotted skin and blood stuck to the toilet bowl. The combined incidents shook me and I called out to Renee, in a moment she was over my shoulder, gently taking the toilet brush from my hand, "I'll clean it," she said as she steered me toward the hall. I was dizzy and nauseated and so very glad to be leaving. I took a deep breath, determined not to lose the momentum of traveling on to a better place.

The "ups" of rebuilding were sure to be accompanied by some "downs", and I was sure to get my fair share. One afternoon I sat in traffic, the familiar fog had once again settled in my brain and I wasn't thinking clearly. The light turned green and the Mustang in front of me proceeded through it, I was close behind and turned my head for what felt like a split second, the next thing I knew I crashed into the back of the Mustang.

A young woman jumped out and came to my car to inquire if I was okay, I apologized profusely and confessed that I had no idea what had happened. Her car showed no damage, but mine looked like an open sardine can, the hood had been pushed back like an accordion. The headlights were broken and dangling from their sockets. The owner of the Mustang suggested we pull to the side of the road and wait for the police to arrive. I was embarrassed by what I had just caused.

I called Kim and told her what happened and where I was, "I'm on 76th Street. I have to go, the officer is pulling up." With that I hung up, stepped out of my car and approached the other lady and a kind motorcycle policeman who I recognized as a local who frequented the Robin Hood Lanes, where I had my coffee each morning and knew well of my situation these last few months.

"Oh, no," he said. "You don't need this," I smiled at his empathy. He asked that we retrieve our driver's license, registration and proof of insurance. I returned to my car, rummaged through the glove box and returned with my papers, when I handed them to him, he shot me a puzzled look, "Isn't that what you want?" I asked.

"This will do," he nodded. It was then that I noticed I hadn't handed him my proof of insurance, instead I had given him someone's business card. I was confused and he covered for me.

As we were finishing up the necessary paperwork, Renee pulled up. She had been at the beach when Kim called her and asked that she try and locate me on 76th Street. The officer was extremely kind, "I don't want to write you a ticket, but I may have to." I told him I understood and he could mail it to me if necessary.

He helped us ease back into traffic, my car was a mess, but I could still drive it and preferred to take it to the body shop myself the following day. Renee told me she was a little worried at how spacey I had been lately, "Why don't you call Dr. Newton and ask if the Prozac might be too much for you."

I did as she suggested and told a nurse what had happened that afternoon and wondered if my prescription might be too strong, that evening there was a message on the machine from Dr. Newton, "Madeline, do not take any more Prozac. I repeat, do not take any more Prozac."

Perhaps my immersion into the fog was nothing more than an over prescribed anti-depressant. That was the hope, anyway.

* * * *

The next day Detective Jones called, "I've got a ticket here with your name on it," he said.

"I figured as much," I said. I knew the officer had to give it to the person at fault and that was me. "I understand," I said, "I'll be in to pick it up tomorrow. Please tell the kind officer not to worry, he's just doing his job."

The next day I rented a car and went to pick up the ticket, Detective Jones told me he planned to nominate me for a medal at the next Medal of Valor ceremony. He said it was in recognition of my role in capturing Chesnutt, "There's a nice dinner, you can bring your family."

"No! I don't want one," I was adamant. I felt my harsh response may have hurt Detective Jones' feelings, but I couldn't bring myself to be in the spotlight.

"Why don't you think about it," he said, "it won't be until sometime next year, so you'll have plenty of time to get used to the idea."

We changed the subject and he asked about Michelle and Jeffery, "Are they getting counseling?" I shook my head, "No. They're not—not yet."

"We took your 911 tape to the police convention in Spokane—don't worry, your identity was protected, but it was a hit. Some of the stations want to use it in training, would that be okay with you?" His delivery was gentle, as if he felt I needed to be treated with kid gloves.

"Go ahead," I said.

I left in a hurry, not wanting to linger on the subject of me, the 911 tape or some medal of valor. I had spent the last several days in an attempt to move forward, and it was a slippery slope right back into the throes of depression and thoughts of Chesnutt and the havoc he wrecked on me and my family.

Back in traffic and anxious to get to the café, I wasn't paying attention to the speedometer. I heard a siren and in checking my rear-view mirror, saw a motorcycle with lights flashing. I pulled off the road and stepped out of my car, the officer was the same one who ticketed me for my accident just days earlier, "Madeline! I didn't know it was you! Please slow down."

I could tell he was upset as he pulled up on his bike, lifting the front wheel clear off the road. "I'm sorry," I said, "I'll be more careful."

The accident, the ticket, speeding—I was feeling out of control and I knew that something would have to change, before I crashed again.

* * * *

I had decided to name my new puppy "Chanel". Although I was all moved in thanks to help from Renee, I wasn't planning to sleep at the apartment until I had Chanel with me. Renee's stepfather had picked up some extra locks for my windows and sliding glass door, and Renee, armed with a drill, installed them.

I asked for permission to put in extra shades over my office window, I was paranoid about being watched while counting money from the café. I returned to the Edmonds Police Department and requested to have my gun returned to me. I had no plans to spend one night alone without my gun. Detective Jones seemed surprised when I asked for it, he brought it to me in pieces and it had dried blood on it.

"What am I supposed to do with this?" I asked. "I don't know how to put it together."

He left the room and returned a few moments later, the gun was reassembled and it had been wiped clean.

"Don't ever get rid of it," he said, "we might need to use it for evidence."

"I have no such plans," I said. I was glad to have my gun back, it had saved my life and however small, it gave me a sense of security.

It seemed that everything was in place for me to physically stay at my apartment, Chanel and I hit it off immediately. The connection was strong and instant and I managed to get through my first night in the apartment with her on my bed and my gun within reach. Renee had accompanied me to the apartment and checked all the windows and doors before leaving me there alone with Chanel and she and Kim insisted I call if I found I was too scared to stay the night. I had decided, however, it was time to move on from Kim's couch. I deserved a place to call my own and now, with Chanel, I felt I could.

Along with the joy Chanel brought, my infatuation with her would bring its share of grief. One afternoon, while admiring her in the seat next to me, I swiped a pole backing out of a parking stall. I drove directly to the body-shop I had picked my car up from just a week earlier. The owner was surprised to see me in there yet again, "How did this happen?" he asked.

I opened the car door and pointed to Chanel, "I've fallen in love," I smiled.

"Oh my," he said. "You have to take her inside and show my wife. She'll love her." I did show his wife, and she did fall instantly in love with Chanel, as did anyone who met her. While the bill for the car repair stung a little, Chanel seemed to make everything a little less painful.

Things were beginning to calm down, but I did find I'd lapse into the fog again from time to time. I was locking my keys in the car at least once or twice a week and AAA was starting to charge me since I had exceeded the allowable number of calls to unlock my car. I had a few extra sets made and left them with Kim and Renee.

While my new direction included lapses in memory, fender benders and a speeding ticket or two, it also included Chanel. She was making me feel happier than I had since the attack, she was my baby and required all my love and attention; demanded it, really. I'd discovered a new purpose, a four-legged ball of white fluff that reintroduced me to love.

CHAPTER 19 – TED

"He played the King as though under momentary apprehension that someone else was about to play the ace."

~*Eugene Field*

"Ted goes to church every Sunday, he's a good Christian," Jaqueline said.

Jaqueline worked at the bank where I did business nearly every day. She seemed adamant that I meet her friend who'd had his heart broken by a failed engagement.

"I'm really not interested in dating right now," I said.

"But, Ted's really a nice guy," she insisted. I wanted to ask, "If he's so great, why aren't you dating him?" but I kept that thought to myself. It had been three months since the attack and I'd grown accustomed to people intent on making decisions on my behalf. I knew they meant well, but I found myself getting a little irritated that I was rarely asked what I wanted.

Jaqueline was persistent and I found my resistance waning. "I'll only meet for coffee," I told her one especially exhausting afternoon, "and you have to be there with me." Her grin was wide as she promised, "You won't be disappointed."

I was determined to get the meeting over with so she would stop harassing me every time I went in to make a deposit. I didn't want Ted to have my phone number, so Jaqueline played matchmaker and called to let me know the coffee date was set.

I canceled the first attempt, no real reason, I was busy, apprehensive and less than interested, but Jaqueline insisted we reschedule and arranged a new time. I felt obliged to keep the appointment, but I was determined to make it quick and formal, "No dinner," I stated. "Just coffee."

The day arrived and I asked Renee to drive me to the restaurant, run some errands and return to pick me up in exactly forty-five minutes. A waiting ride meant I had no choice but to leave when Renee arrived, no matter how our meeting had progressed. If I wanted to see him again, I was sure that could be arranged.

I entered the restaurant and Jaqueline was nowhere to be seen, only a rather loud and brazen man at the pay phone. He wasn't my type; the only reason I was aware of his presence was his commanding voice.

Seven minutes had passed when he hung up the phone and approached me, "You must be Maddie," Jaqueline must have given him my nick-name.

"Yes," I said. He introduced himself as Ted and suggested we go sit down. He was about 5'10" tall with thick brown hair. His head appeared too big for his body and he was far less attractive than other men I had dated after my divorce from Tom.

The hostess seated us and he immediately began grilling me with questions about the café; how many employees did I have, where was it located and how long had I been in business.

I was getting a little weary of the interrogation when Jaqueline arrived. She sat down and began spewing information about her day, her work, her children, her church and God knows what else. She monopolized the conversation and soon I looked at my watch, rose from my chair and announced that it was time for me to go.

Ted looked shocked that I had called an end to our meeting so abruptly, "I thought we were going to order something to eat," he said.

"I told Jaqueline I only had forty-five minutes," I said. I wondered why he had let Jaqueline Shanghai our conversation if he was so interested in talking to me, He could have easily interrupted her, if he wanted to, I thought.

"Can I call you?" he asked.

"If you want," I answered, "Jaqueline has my number."

I knew he would get my voice mail and I wouldn't have to return the call, in fact, the silence from my end would be a sure indicator that we were far less than a good fit.

Renee was waiting for me and I hopped in the car, "Let's get out of here," I said. Just then Ted and Jaqueline exited the restaurant into the parking lot, "That's him," I said.

She watched him walk to his car, "He's not a bad looking guy, Maddie," she said and then turned to me, "how did it go?"

"I don't know," I said, "Jaqueline talked the entire time. Let's go get something to eat." Renee laughed and started the car. I was fairly certain I'd seen the last of Ted.

* * * *

I was expecting a call from one of my employees about a pastry order, so when the phone rang, I didn't think twice about picking it up.

"Hello?" I said, anxious to deal with the business at hand. It was Ted.

"I was hoping we'd have more time to talk," he said, "Jaqueline certainly has a way of stealing the conversation."

He went on to ask if I had plans for the weekend, I stalled for time. I really had no desire to get to know him better and I had no real reason as to why.

"You don't have to marry him," said Kim when I told her and Renee about Ted's invitation to the car races. "It sounds like fun, after all you've been through, you could use a little of that. You should go."

I considered it for a minute, shrugged my shoulders and said, "Okay, I'll go."

Ted was a regional sales manager for a national chain of funeral home. He sold burial plots and arranged funerals. I tried to look past the morbidity of his chosen profession and see the positive side of his demeanor. He opened my car door, a plus, his car was neat and clean, two points, there was a Bible on the back seat, hmmm, he's religious and seems to know how to treat a lady.

He took my hand as we walked toward the grandstand. I wasn't crazy about the hand-holding, minus two points.

The races had already begun when we found our seats. I had never been to a car race before and while it was enjoyable, the fumes got to me. We ended the evening with corndogs and scones at the food booths and then Ted took me back to my car. We had met in my old townhouse development, I didn't want him to know where I lived, just yet.

He was observant enough not to try and kiss me, but he did ask me out for the following evening. I told him I had plans, but that didn't deter him.

"Come to church with me on Sunday," he asked. "A brunch will follow the service."

I accepted his invitation and we parted ways.

We went to church that Sunday and brunched at a nearby restaurant. He asked if I'd like to take a walk along the Kirkland Waterfront, "Another time," I said, "I've got some work to do for the café." He told me he'd call that evening.

The calls were frequent, he called daily to ask me out. I made excuses as to why I couldn't see him, the truth was—I just wasn't interested. I met an old friend for dinner and Ted wanted details, "How did you meet him?" and "How long have you known him?"...I began to get weary of the constant questions.

As time went on, Ted would become more and more annoyed if he wasn't included in my daily plans. Plans with Michelle or Kim and Renee would spark a barrage of questions. An angry undertone would creep into his voice and I found myself just "going along", as if he were somehow running my life.

One day an employee of mine phoned me to say that a bouquet of roses had just been delivered, I was curious as to who sent them and went by the café, only to find that the roses were from Ted. I felt embarrassed and slightly annoyed. My employee smiled, "Who's the special guy," she asked.

I didn't find Ted special and I was a little sickened to think that he was attempting to put himself as such. I took the flowers to Kim and Renee's and told them they may as well enjoy them. I did the right thing and called Ted to thank him, he responded with, "Beautiful roses for a beautiful lady." He went on to ask what I was doing that evening, I begged off by telling him I was tired. The real reason was I wanted the pursuit to slow down. I wasn't feeling comfortable at all.

That night Ted called to say goodnight and casually inquired as to my plans for the next day. "I've got an appointment with my therapist," I said.

"Is he Christian," he asked.

"I believe he and his wife attend your church," I was a little taken aback when he asked if he could accompany me to the appointment, "I guess that'd be alright." I wondered if perhaps getting Dr. Jantz's opinion on Ted might help me feel more comfortable.

The following morning Ted was elated to see me, we had lunch and he told me all about an upcoming annual retreat for his company's sales staff and their significant others. It was to take place at the Rosario Resort in San Juan Islands.

He asked if I'd be his guest, "I'm dying to introduce you to my staff." I told him I wasn't comfortable with going and there was no way I could spend an entire weekend. He seemed disappointed, but I sensed he wasn't about to give up quite so easily.

I spent the first half hour of my appointment alone with Dr. Jantz, I shared with him how things were going and that Ted seemed to be pushing and shoving his way into my life.

"He's a good Christian, but the flowers, calls and now the offer for a weekend away seem a little aggressive to me."

"Let me see how he strikes me," said Dr. Jantz.

Ted joined us and came across as personable and talkative, he spoke about church, his Amish upbringing and how he had become a Christian. I felt he had seemed to win over Dr. Jantz, but I was still apprehensive. He spoke about our relationship, how he hoped it would evolve to marriage and how he didn't believe in pre-marital sex, "It's in the Bible," he said, "no one said doing the right thing is easy." Both he and Dr. Jantz laughed, but I was uncomfortable as to where the conversation had gone, I had only known him for two weeks.

When we left the office, Ted mentioned again how disappointed he was that I wouldn't go on the retreat. "Maybe for a day," I said, "but there's no way I can be away from the café for an entire weekend."

He took me back to my car and asked if we could have dinner that evening, I begged off with an excuse that I had work to do. Within two hours of our parting, he was on the phone with me, "I checked with Kenmore Air and we can get you to Rosario for the day," he said. Once again his persistence was wearing me down, "Okay," I said, "I'll get Renee to cover for me."

Two days later I saw Dr. Jantz again and told him of my plan to spend a day at the retreat, "It's good for you to get away," he said. "Go and enjoy yourself."

I wasn't convinced that was possible, I was feeling pushed, pulled and prodded—coming on the heels of Chesnutt, they weren't exactly welcome feelings.

* * * *

Later that evening, Ted and I had plans for dinner. Neither one of us were very hungry, so we decided to walk around Seattle until our appetites kicked in. Ted liked to hold my hand as we walked and this night was no different, as we walked by a jewelry store Ted said he'd like to take a peek inside.

Ted asked the clerk to see two ruby and diamond rings. "Here, try them on," he said.

I humored him and tried them on, "They look beautiful on you," he said, "which one would you like?"

I was stunned, "Why would you buy me a ring?" I asked.

"I'm serious about us, Maddie. I want to show you that I have no intention of dating anyone else," he said.

"I don't need you to buy me a ring to tell me that," I said, "I know you're not seeing anyone else."

My protests were disregarded, he picked one and purchased it without even asking the price. The clerk said it could be fitted and ready the following day.

"Just in time for Rosario, I want you to wear it when you meet me there," he said.

"Look Maddie," he touched my face and my instinct was to pull back, "this is only the beginning. I have a lot to offer you and I intend to start right away."

At dinner he declared his devotion to me, "I've been looking for someone to spend the rest of my life with and you're it." I was cautious, I'd known this man less than a month, "Things are going a little fast, don't you think?" I asked.

"When it's right, there is no time. I'd like to see us married before the end of the year," he was adamant and I was very confused. It had been less than four months since the attack and I was still in shock, I felt dazed by his statements and I didn't have the wherewithal to argue or pay heed to the red flags. It was as if I was a spectator, watching my life unfold with no say as to how it was to proceed.

I picked up the ring the following day and flew to Rosario. Ted was thrilled to have me there and showed it in the manner in which he introduced me—especially to other men, "Isn't she beautiful?" I didn't feel beautiful and felt my face flush every time he said it.

The days went by and Ted made a point of calling often. He was constantly asking me to spare time for him, he wanted to be involved in every aspect of my life. The business was demanding; there were employee issues to deal with, adjusting to my new apartment and Ted's constant barrage of questions about what I was doing with my day, who I was with and what were my plans for the next day and the next after that. I was drowning in a sea of confusion.

A few days later, Ted would ask if he could kiss me. I had been grateful that he had taken his time in getting to any physical contact.

"I've been wanting to kiss you for a while," he said. He took my face in his hands the way Chesnutt had and I pulled them away, his kiss was awkward and ill at ease.

"I love you, Maddie," he said. "Will you marry me?"

The look on my face must have been a combination of fear and horror, because he followed it instantly with, "You don't have to answer right away. Take a couple of days."

"I think that would be best," I said.

The following day, roses arrived at the cafe. The note said, "I look forward to a lifetime of happiness with you. I love you. Ted."

My employee told me I'd be a fool to pass up a man like that, "He adores you," she said. I couldn't help my feelings, I wasn't head over heels in love with Ted, maybe it was the rape that had numbed my ability to feel that kind of love again, maybe I was a different person thanks to Chesnutt.

I came clean with Ted and told him how I felt.

"Let's just get married and everything will fall into place," he said.

I thought about my longing to have a normal life once more, I thought about my inability to feel safe—my longing for a meaningful relationship.

"Yes," I said. "I'll marry you.

I had no idea I had just agreed to, once again, become the victim.

CHAPTER 20 – THE ENGAGEMENT

"I'm living life as best I can—but I'm not exempt from failure and making bad choices."

~*Unknown*

We began our search for a home to call our own, I had no desire to leave Edmonds. The Edmonds Police Department made me feel safe, even months after the attack they continued to stay in touch with me. We found a custom home still in the building stages. It was built by a renowned local contractor and we fell in love with it.

I was busier than ever now, rushing around, picking out carpeting, lighting, tile and appliances for the house. I was still experiencing my moments of "fogginess", I'd stop at green lights and run red lights. I was constantly being honked at and did end up back at the body shop after yet another mishap, I nicknamed my car the bondo-mobile. I wrote my clumsiness off to nerves and the impending change. It seemed I hadn't had a home since I was married to Tom. I was hopeful that I was on my way to a normal life once again.

Ted insisted that my name be put on the deed of the house, even though I didn't contribute to the $70,000.00 down payment. He said it was fair as the café was worth at least that much and since we would be married soon, that would become marital property. He found that to be fair and equitable. The house was scheduled to be completed by the middle of November, well before our wedding day. Ted wanted us to move in together as soon as the house was done. I reminded him of his intent to do everything according to "the Christian way". He promised to sleep downstairs until we were married. I opted to keep my apartment and stick with the original plan.

Ted's behavior was erratic. He demanded my time constantly and I knew it had to be devoted to the café and occasionally my friends who had been there for me so often and for so long. "I'm not about to give up my friends," I told him.

"Yes, but I want to spend time with you. I wish we were already married," he stated.

I should have read into the meaning of his words right there and then, if we were married, then he could control me.

Tickets to "Cats" for Kim, Renee and I turned into a battle about his wanting to accompany me to the play.

"The tickets were bought a long time ago," I said, "I can't very well ask either of them to give up their ticket for you." I suggested he get together with his motorcycle friends and have dinner out somewhere. I wasn't into his bike or his friends and thought it would be a good opportunity for him to see them without me.

The morning of the play, Ted called me to wish me a good morning, "You know, I love you," he said, "but understand that no man would want you after what happened to you."

I was shocked, how could he be so insensitive, my response was swift, "Really? Well that's strange, all the men who come into the café say they would hope their wives or girlfriends would do exactly as I did."

He became quiet and although he didn't apologize, he didn't mention it again.

The play was wonderful and my time with Kim and Renee was much needed. I got home a little after midnight and there were four messages from Ted, each more frantic than the one before it.

I called him and he picked up, "Hi, are you okay?" I asked.

"Well I guess so, where have you been?" he asked.

"Ted, you knew I was at the play with Kim and Renee," I was beginning to get annoyed.

"This late?" This didn't feel like someone who missed me, it felt more like someone who didn't trust me. I wondered why he would want to marry me if he lacked the trust that was so necessary.

"The play ran until 11:30 and we got home just about midnight. I took Chanel out and just got back inside. What did you do tonight?" I tried to shift the conversation, only to regret it.

"Since you went to see "Cats" without me, I thought I'd chase some pussy."

I was shocked. "I'm kidding," he said. I couldn't believe those words came from the man who claimed to be such a good Christian. He delighted in the fact that his comment upset me. He was obviously jealous of my time with Kim and Renee and this was nothing more than payback.

Additional awakenings to my journey to disaster would include an anniversary lunch for my Aunt JoAnn put on by my Uncle John. I had told Ted that Aunt JoAnn had passed away shortly before their 50th wedding anniversary and that the lunch was to commemorate their anniversary and honor her life. A place was set in her honor and Ted gestured toward the empty chair and asked, "When will JoAnn be arriving?" I was put off by his insensitivity, "She died, that's why we're here." I was trying desperately to like this man who was to become my husband, but I was finding it more and more difficult.

His actions continued, he'd be a complete jerk and then call the next day as if nothing had happened. He'd send roses or a gift and I was expected to simply erase his antics from my memory. I began to worry about my decision and suggested we have some joint sessions with Dr. Jantz.

Ted became jealous of Chanel. She required a lot of my time in training, but she was worth every moment. She made me feel safe, I could trust her to alert me in the middle of the night and that was important to me after my horrible experience. I needed her and she needed me and Ted was not a part of that equation.

Next he made statements about my friends, "I don't think we should associate with people who don't go to church every Sunday."

"I'm not going to give up my friends because they don't go to church on Sunday," I said. "I've got friends whose character outweighs many who go to church on Sunday. It's how you behave to the rest of the world the other six days that counts." I braved my fear, "I think we should reconsider getting married," I said. "Let's respect our differences."

His attitude would change instantly, "It's not that big a deal," he'd say. But my guard was up and my determination to protect my non-church-going friends was strong. I would not be swayed and abandon people I knew were good to the core. The subject would be raised again and again; each time he'd become angry that he was unable to change my mind. I simply learned to tune him out.

* * * *

Ted asked if I had a preference for who would perform the wedding ceremony, immediately my former pastor from Lake Tapps Community Church came to mind. Tom and I had attended the church for many years and I grew quite fond of him.

I contacted him and he invited Ted and I to his office. He told Ted that he had known me for years and would like to see me happily married once again, but in order to feel comfortable about performing the ceremony, he'd like to learn more about Ted.

Ted was more than thrilled to sell himself as a good Christian, he spoke of his desire to refrain from sex until after we were married, in accordance with the Bible. The Pastor asked Ted about his previous marriages; he had been married twice before and both ended in divorce.

Ted blamed the first failed marriage on his ex-wife's affair with another man, but he was far vaguer about the reasons behind the demise of his second marriage. The pastor then asked if Ted knew the whereabouts of his second wife and Ted told him he had lost contact with her.

The pastor said he'd like to do a little research before agreeing to perform the ceremony and asked if he could call the following week with his decision. We thanked him and left. Later that week, the pastor called and left a voice mail saying he didn't feel comfortable marrying Ted and I and if I would give him a call back, he'd be happy to explain. I didn't call him back until three years later, when I penned this book. I felt it was necessary to find out why he had declined to marry us.

"I just felt something wasn't right," he said, "I found Ted egotistical." Looking back, I wish I had bothered to call him the moment I heard his message, I would likely have listened to him.

* * * *

We flew to Pennsylvania to meet Ted's family; his daughter and her family, his brother and his parents. Everyone was hospitable, but his mother seemed unhappy, barely cracking a smile our entire visit.

A tour of his hometown would take us past his first girlfriend's house, "Are you jealous?" he asked. I was a little perplexed, "Why would I be jealous?" I asked.

He seemed disappointed, "I'd be jealous if it were your first boyfriend's house," he said.

"No Ted, I'm not jealous. That was a long time ago." He seemed agitated, but dropped the subject. I found the whole exchange strange and put it out of my mind. I tended to tuck away all the oddities that came with Ted, I turned a blind eye or a deaf ear to his weird ticks and comments, with no understanding as to why I chose to ignore red flag after red flag.

Upon returning home I had lunch with my best friend, Patti, "Why the rush?" she asked, "Are you pregnant?" I laughed, "No!" I said, but her question made me stop and think. Perhaps I was rushing headlong into disaster. I wondered if I was really just trying to escape the past four months as fast as possible; perhaps a new house, a new husband and a new lease on life seemed the only way out of the tunnel I'd been shoved into since the attack.

My actions felt forced, my desire to put aside everything about Ted that felt awkward and troublesome, bothered me. Why was I trying so hard to make him fit into my idea of what a good man was?

Things began to get even odder as Ted began pressuring me for sex.

"Abstaining was your idea!" I said, "Perhaps we should discuss it with Dr. Jantz." His hands flew into the air, "I don't even know if you're sexually attracted to me!"

His tantrum was short-lived, but it was decided that I would continue to see Dr. Jantz on my own and Ted would get his own counselor, we had been seeing Dr. Jantz together, but now I was feeling the contradictions I was noting from Ted were troubling.

He'd judge people for drinking and then drink with his co-workers, he didn't want to be seen drinking in public with me, but insisted it was okay for us to drink in private. He seemed to constantly judge others as to whether they were a "good Christian", or not.

One afternoon while we were arranging furniture in the new house, Ted asked me how I felt about abortion. I said I felt it should be legal. His face flushed and he became livid, "No wife of mine is going to believe in abortion!" he yelled.

"A victim of rape or incest should not have to carry the reminder of the crime committed against her!" I was adamant in my belief and had no intention of debating the issue. He obviously saw something in my face that said arguing the issue would be futile, and he backed off.

It was becoming more and more clear that our differences were far greater than any similarities—but I was continuing headlong into the brick wall. Deep down I knew it and I couldn't bring myself to stop the madness.

A few days later some friends of Ted's came into town for a long weekend. He said they were, "good Christians" and he was sure I would like them. I was getting tired of him labeling who was and wasn't a "good Christian", but I kept my mouth shut.

The two couples arrived in town and they seemed nice and happy to meet me. We had reservations for dinner the first evening and I rode with them in their car to show them where the restaurant was, Ted followed in his car. They told me of their trip into town and their extended lunch at Pioneer Square. I could smell alcohol on their breath as they laughed and told off-color and racially charged jokes that made me instantly uncomfortable.

The jokes continued through dinner and I noticed Ted laughing right along with them. The smoking, drinking and telling of dirty jokes were in direct opposition of what Ted had been preaching to me about "good Christians", and yet here he was with these people he called his "best friends".

The conversation turned to my café and Ted's friend asked how long I had owned it, Ted chimed in that he was anxious to expand it, "I'd like to franchise our business," he said. I was stunned. The café was mine, it always was and it always would be. I had no intention of making it marital property. I suddenly felt control slipping away, was this his way of getting payback for putting my name on the house—against my wishes?

I silently vowed that I would somehow protect my business. The hypocrisy, the judgment, the quoting of scripture—it was my doctor who would hand me four quotes of scripture after I confessed my fear of Ted's ways, and say, "Next time he starts in, have him read these quotes from the Bible. They all refer to the dangers of judging others."

While I left my appointment feeling somewhat better, I recalled a quote about those who pray loudest, "Such prayer is not real prayer, but empty words meant for the ears of other people".

Ted's words, his judgment, his meaningless definition of a "good Christian" were anything but, real prayer.

CHAPTER 21 – GETTING MARRIED—ANYWAY

"Sooner or later everyone sits down to a banquet of consequences."
~Robert Louis Stevenson

Detective Bruce told me I was moving too fast. Michelle told me she didn't plan on coming to my New Year's Eve wedding. Mike took me out for a friendly dinner and said, point blank, "Don't marry him."

I was on a roller coaster of confusion, Mike said he still loved me and while he planned to spend Christmas in San Francisco with friends he begged me to reconsider, "Wait until I get back from California and we can be together." I reasoned that if Mike truly loved me, he wouldn't go to California in the first place. He'd stay and convince me to dodge the bullet that would become life with Ted.

Ted had gone to Pennsylvania to spend some holiday time with his family, he called every night and every night I'd had dinner with Mike. He was intoxicating to me, he always looked handsome and I felt safe in his company. Something I hadn't yet felt with Ted, I wrote if off to the fact that we hadn't yet slept together and figured that as soon as we did, those feelings of love, loyalty and attraction would follow.

The night before Mike left for San Francisco we had our last dinner together. We hugged one another and cried. He then continued to call me daily, expressing his love and causing me to become more confused and even more depressed.

Ted returned from Pennsylvania one week before our wedding was to take place. He was very excited, taking care of all the last minute details. He had hired movers to move my furniture in the new house in time for me to entertain my family for Christmas. He bought me a new cell phone and took it upon himself to change my number. Mike wouldn't be able to call me on my cell and although he left messages on my home phone, I decided not to respond to them.

I was going to marry Ted and I would have to get a handle on how everyone else's behavior was affecting me. I had convinced Michelle to attend the wedding, but she said if Ted so much as touched her, she'd leave at once, "He gives me the creeps, Mom," she said.

On Christmas eve, I picked up a prime rib, set the table and put the finishing touches on our new home before returning to my apartment. Ted and I had bought a lovely tree and as I looked around, I could see this beautiful house becoming my home.

Mom, Dad, Michelle, Jeffery and Lily all showed up Christmas Day. My good friend Julie had a change of plans so she was able to join us as well. We ate dinner and then opened presents. Afterward, I went to the kitchen to prepare dessert. Julie needed to make a phone call, so I asked Michelle to show her to the study. When I returned with dessert, Michelle and Julie weren't around, I found them in the study with the French doors shut.

"What are you doing," I asked as I opened the door. "Mom, shut the door," Michelle said.

"I've just got a feeling about him," said Julie. My heart sunk, here I was just six days away from my wedding and there was no stopping now.

"He's hiding something," said Julie, "I don't know what, but he's hiding something."

"Don't be ridiculous, come and have dessert," I forced a smile. "Everything's fine." If only I believed it.

After dessert I walked in on Ted and Julie in the kitchen, his face was pale, with a blank, uneasy stare. I eventually corned Julie and asked her what they were talking about.

"He's hiding something," she said.

"How do you know?" I asked.

"I just know," she answered.

The next several days were full of holiday gatherings and preparation for the wedding, at one party, an old co-worker sat next to me on the couch and extended his arm across the back of the couch. We visited while Ted kept peeking around the corner at us, I invited him to join us and he did, but had little to say...until we got to the car.

Renee was with us and sat in back. I don't think she was prepared for the jealous rage that Ted would erupt in.

"How dare you let that guy put his arm around you?!"

"Ted, relax, Larry's just a friend. He has a girlfriend; you'll meet her at the wedding! Besides, his arm wasn't around me, it was on the back of the couch!" I said. I was embarrassed for Renee to witness the stupid exchange.

"Well, maybe we should just call off the wedding!"

He said it, not me. I held my breath for a moment, maybe I would be off the hook after all.

His tirade was followed by a quick cool down and an immediate apology. I glanced at Renee in the backseat, her eyes said everything I felt.

Ted took Renee home and dropped me at my apartment. I laid in bed that night wondering how foolish Ted must be feeling for his grossly unwarranted behavior, and then I realized, he probably didn't give it a second thought. He was comfortable with who he was, although no one else felt that way—no one at all.

* * * *

New Year's Eve arrived. I had a 2p.m. nail appointment and a 5p.m. hair appointment. I was to be at The Lakes Club no later than 7p.m. I hadn't had a chance to eat all day and Renee was driving me so that I could leave with Ted and spend the first night in our new home with my husband.

"Are you hungry," Renee asked.

"I don't know," I answered.

We stopped at a restaurant and as we waited to order, she looked hard into my eyes, "Maddie, you don't have to do this." My gaze dropped, I couldn't find the words to justify what I was about to do.

"We can leave, right now," she said. I shook my head, "All those people," I said. "They'll be waiting for me."

"With all that you've been through, all those people will understand," she said.

I so appreciated what she was trying to do, but I couldn't bring myself to admit that it had all been a big mistake. I wasn't strong enough to say I had wasted even more time and energy on the wrong man, the wrong house, the wrong circumstances. I couldn't bring myself to say that I should have been spending the past four months continuing to heal.

"What time is it?" I asked, "It's 6:45," she answered.

I took a deep breath, "Let's order," I said.

We arrived at The Lakes Club at 7:15pm for an 8:00 wedding. There would be no turning back.

* * * *

The bridal coordinator was glad to see me and whisked me away to the bridal dressing room where I would change clothes and emerge in a light pink and white brocade bridal suit with matching beaded hat. Renee assisted with the finishing touches and I was ready.

My parents arrived and came into the room to greet me, "You look beautiful," my mother said. The bridal coordinator was anxious to get me on my way to holy matrimony and coaxed my mother to her seat and me to the altar on my father and Jeffery's arms.

My father and Jeffery walked me up the aisle where the minister and Ted were waiting. I stopped in my tracks, "I can't..." I said.

"What's the matter?" my father asked.

I couldn't tell him this was wrong, Ted was wrong, this whole affair was wrong! I just stood there in a dead stop, "I can't go in."

Jeffery tried to lighten things up, "Get her a drink," he said, "she'll be okay." The bridal coordinator prodded me toward the altar, "You'll be fine," she said.

I stumbled in with my father and my son at my side, Ted gasped when he saw me, I was completely disoriented. I stood next to Ted in a daze as vows were exchanged, it was all a blur. Suddenly we were married and as I turned to the witnesses of our marriage, I realized that they looked far happier than I felt.

The wedding dinner consisted of various pasta dishes and Ceaser salad and preceded the cake that was adorned with flowers that matched my bouquet. Guests danced as a disc-jockey spun record after record. At midnight, he played Auld Lang Syne to welcome in the new year. Many wanted to stay and continue dancing, finally, by 1:00am, the DJ called the last dance. Ted and I left at 1:30am to spend our first night together.

On our way home, the interrogation began. "Where did you go with Larry?" he asked.

"What are you talking about?" I asked.

"I saw you and Larry leave the reception hall together, then I couldn't find you. Where did you go?" His accusatory tone was disturbing.

"Barbara, Joanie and Renee went out to have a cigarette. I joined them and Larry came out a few minutes later. We were never alone." I felt bad for having to defend myself or Larry in any way.

"Why didn't you just come out?" He didn't answer me, he just took my hand and in that instance my fear was confirmed, I had made a terrible mistake in marrying Ted.

Ted lay naked in the bed when I came out of the bathroom. I slipped under the covers and joined him in an odd, obligatory way. He wasn't a good lover, his kisses were too hard and he held me in a way that felt suffocating, I instinctively moved his hands from my face.

"My baby's so hot," he said as if speaking to an onlooker, "isn't she hot?" I was more than a little disturbed by this strange behavior. When it was over, he fell asleep and I just laid there in disbelief.

What had I done?

* * * *

Things began to get even more strange. Chanel would stay close on my heels when Ted was home, more than once I walked in the room to find Chanel on her back and Ted's hands on her genitals. When he saw me, he quickly moved his hands to her belly and began to rub it. He looked embarrassed, as if he'd been caught.

Chanel had slept on my bed since the day I brought her home, but Ted now insisted she stay on the floor. She had a terrible time adjusting and cried most of the night.

Making love continued to be weird, Ted would make feverish comments to no one in particular, "My baby is so hot," he was anything but gentle and his kisses reminded me of Chesnutt. I asked him many times to stop his aggressiveness.

One morning, soon after the wedding, I woke at 6a.m. to find Ted entering our bedroom.

"Where were you?" I asked.

"I couldn't sleep so I went in Calvin's room." Calvin was Ted's son who would visit every few months, so we made a room for him in the basement.

I'd often wake during the night and find Ted gone. I assumed he couldn't sleep and had retreated to Calvin's room.

One evening he went for a walk, it was late and I declined to accompany him, "It's too late," I said. "It's dark." He went anyway, saying he was determined to lose weight. He returned less than an hour later, "I'm scared," he said.

"Why?" I asked. I was curled up on the couch watching a movie, Chanel was on my lap and made no move to greet him.

"I was walking and there was a car full of boys. They followed me and I hid behind a tree at a nearby house, the owners of the home drove up and their headlights shined on me. I ran all the way home."

Ted wasn't out of breath and I asked why he didn't bother to call me from the neighbor's phone, "I'm sure they would have been fine with you calling me to come and get you." He was silent and I was confused, his story didn't match his actions.

Soon, Ted was going for walks by himself almost nightly. He was in counseling and one Sunday, on our way to church, he told me he had asked his counselor if he could force me to have sex.

I was stunned, "That's rape," I said.

"I didn't get married to refrain from sex," he said. "But consider yourself safe, my counselor said forcing anyone, including a spouse, is considered rape."

After all I'd been through, I couldn't believe the man I married had been seeking permission to rape me.

"Yes," I agreed, "that would be rape."

* * * *

Ted ventured off on a five-day trip, part business and part to see his daughter and baby granddaughter. I told him I thought it was a nice idea and I was actually looking forward to the time to catch up in the café and visit with Renee and Kim.

On the third evening, Renee and I decided to watch the Sonics playoff game in a local sports bar. There was a ten-dollar cover, plus dinner, but the atmosphere was fun and the change of scenery, welcome.

I checked my voice mail from the bar and Ted had left a message to call him at his daughter's in Pennsylvania. I called from a pay phone, it was 9:30pm in Pennsylvania, "You're at a bar?" he asked.

"It's a sports bar, we're just here to watch the Sonics," I said. "You're always going out to dinner and drinks when you're out of town," I reminded him, "I never complain about it."

I reassured him that he had nothing to worry about and he calmed down. We chatted about his granddaughter and he promised he'd call in the morning.

Renee and I ended up visiting my friend, Lauren a little later, she was going through a bad break-up and just needed company. We took Chanel with us, she seemed to ease even the toughest of circumstances, and this was no exception. We visited and played with Chanel until Lauren felt a little better, then headed for home.

Renee left for her place and I was getting ready for bed when I noticed the light blinking on the answering machine. Ted called several times and left several messages, each more distraught than the one before it. I looked at the clock and realized it was well after three a.m. in Pennsylvania and decided to wait and phone him in the morning. Just then, the phone rang.

It was Ted, "Where have you been?" He was angry and upset and sounded like he'd been crying.

"Relax Ted, we were with Lauren," I said.

"Who's Lauren?" he demanded, "Funny you've never spoken of her before. Have I met her? I don't remember meeting her!"

"It's late," I said, "go to sleep and we'll talk tomorrow." He went on to tell me he'd spoken with his daughter about my going to a bar and she said it was no big deal.

I felt incredulous, I didn't need his daughter's seal of approval to go and watch my team at a local bar, and I didn't need Ted's permission to be an adult out with friends.

The next morning, he called to apologize.

The following day I had lunch with a friend who would be moving to Alaska, she called to tell me she was running late and that gave me a chance to poke my head into a local photography studio while I waited. Ted had said he'd wanted a picture of me to put on his desk, so I made an appointment and laid down a deposit for a photo shoot the following Monday. My plan was to surprise Ted.

* * * *

Ted returned from Pennsylvania and things began to get even more weird. He'd stop in the café unannounced and if I wasn't there, he'd demand to know where I was. I felt bad for my employees who would have to put up with his third degree questioning. I became angry more than once and asked that he please not make the employees uncomfortable.

He'd hired a maid service to clean our home and while inspecting their work, I noticed the blinds on the sliding glass doors in the family room and in the guest bedroom had been bent and creased. I wondered why, this was a brand new house and I thought it strange—I would soon discover how strange.

I decided to hold off on the photo shoot until things improved, I was angry at Ted for interrogating my employee about my whereabouts. One such encounter was over a simple spontaneous breakfast with Renee, I was hungry after my shift and asked her to meet me at a local restaurant. Why Ted felt the need to know my every move was unsettling.

The following Sunday the studio called my cell phone as we were on our way to church, they were confirming my appointment for the following day. I didn't want to cancel the appointment with Ted just a few feet away, I told them I would call them back.

We went to church and when it was over my cell phone rang again, this time it was Alisha from the café, she asked if I could please come and relieve her for a break. She was hungry and needed to use the bathroom. When I hung up the phone, Ted exploded, "I knew it! You're seeing someone! What's with all the calls?" His attack was completely unwarranted and I was determined to let him know how foolish he was being, "Ted! That was Alisha! She needs me to stop by the café and give her a break."

We drove directly to the café, not another word was said. I covered Alisha's break and Ted helped by filling the water canisters. When Alisha returned we left for home.

"I know you're seeing someone!" We hadn't been back in the car for more than a minute when he started on me. "What about that call this morning? That was him, wasn't it?" His accusations were incredible and unfounded.

"You're sick," I said as I pulled proof of my deposit to the studio from my purse. "I had a photo shoot scheduled. I was going to get my picture done for your desk, but now I don't want it. You've been sneaking around questioning my employees about my whereabouts."

"Bullshit!" he said. Even with the receipt as proof, he refused to believe me.

I lost my mind, "Do you know what people do to people like you?" I shouted. I had never hit a man besides Chesnutt, but I was becoming awfully close now.

He looked at me, his voice full of sarcasm, "You'd probably shoot me if you could."

That was it, I could take no more, "I'm not going to help put you out of your misery, you can do that all by yourself, but what I can say is that this marriage is over! I've had enough! You need help!"

He pulled into the driveway and I quickly headed inside, my plan was to pack a bag, grab Chanel and get out of there as soon as I was able. I called Renee, "He's nuts, I can't stay here. He needs help!"

I told her I'd be over within the hour.

CHAPTER 22 – RED FLAGS

"It has been a distressing, shocking, unworthy, immoral marriage."
~Madeline Morehouse

Ted chased me up the stairs, "Where are you going?" he asked.

"I have to get out of here," I said, "I want a divorce! You need help!" I wasn't sure if I should tell him where I planned to go. I didn't want him to follow me to Kim and Renee's.

He began to cry, "I know I need help," he sobbed, "please don't go. I was afraid I'd lose my job if I checked into a hospital."

He sat on the bed, his head in his hands, "Now I'm losing my marriage." I continued to pack, I wasn't feeling the empathy he desired, I felt he was just trying to lure me into staying.

"Just call the Crisis Clinic," I said. I gave him a forced hug, "Call me on my cell if you want a ride to the hospital." I made my way to the door and turned one last time, "Get some help, Ted." With that I walked out.

Three hours later Ted called to tell me he was driving himself to the hospital near Northgate.

* * * *

The next day I drove to the hospital to visit him, I felt an obligation since he had made the effort to check himself in. I'd never been to a place like this, it felt odd to walk past people who looked perfectly normal, but weren't allowed to leave on their own accord.

Ted was called to the lobby to greet me and from there we would proceed to an area where we would wait to meet with his counselor. The meeting was intense, Ted exploded more than once. The first time was about Renee and I going to a bar to watch the Sonics game.

"You can't control what other people do," said the counselor, "It sounds as if your wife was completely within her rights to enjoy an evening with a friend."

Ted was livid, "No wife of mine is going to a bar!"

The counselor took a breath and with a slight shake of his head said, "Ted, this is your issue—not hers."

Ted went on to complain that I hadn't added his name to the café, "Your name is on the house!" he yelled.

I came to my own defense stating, "Look, I never wanted my name on the house. You insisted on putting it there when we weren't even married! Take my name off, I don't care, but the café is mine."

To be honest, I wouldn't have had a problem putting Ted's name on the business, but his odd, controlling ways spooked me into wanting to protect myself. The business was my livelihood, to put his name on it and afford him fifty percent of its worth scared me.

When I left the hospital, Ted handed me a shirt that he had made in a craft class, it had my name on it and below that a slogan that read, "Free at last - By Ted". I could only surmise that he felt he owned me. The slogan suggested that I was his; mind, body and soul and he was ready to release me. Frankly I didn't believe that he was freeing me in any way. He was a liar and I was beginning to understand how true that was.

* * * *

Ted came home and I was relieved when he decided to sleep in the guest room. Things continued to feel strange to me, the blinds in the guest room become even more bent, when I confronted him about it, he blamed the maids, "It's probably from the vacuum," he surmised. His explanations for anything odd or out of the ordinary were always followed with a shrug of his shoulders and a quick change of subject.

He began doing his own laundry; another odd behavior. I was never one to let it pile up, so there was no reason for him to take that initiative. I also noticed tiny red specks in the washing machine that I wasn't able to identify. I wrote his sudden interest in doing laundry off to the fact that he'd been traveling quite a bit since his return from the hospital.

The following week, I experienced some spotting. Having had a hysterectomy years earlier, I had no idea why this would occur, I feared the worst and made an appointment with Dr. Newton for the following Monday, which also happened to be my birthday.

Sunday morning, I broke my fear to Ted over coffee, "If you haven't already taken out life insurance on me, now might be a good time. I've been spotting for the past few days and I'm concerned it might be cancer." Without missing a beat, Ted quickly changed the subject, "I've been thinking. Maybe we should sell this house and by something on the water."

I was stunned, I had just told him something was terribly wrong and he brings up real-estate, "Ted! Did you hear what I just said?"

"Yes," he said, "I'm going to grab the paper, maybe we can head out today and have a look around the waterfront." I found his dismissiveness to be absurd and as we drove around later in the day looking at houses we didn't need, nor did I want, I realized his manipulative ways had once again won out. Having just voiced my biggest fear, his lack of concern was infuriating—but, I soon found out why.

"You have crabs," said my doctor. It was hardly the birthday surprise I had in mind. A wave of nausea washed over me as I envisioned live insects on my body. The doctor gave me instructions on how to get rid of them, but there was no way to wash away the anger and humiliation I felt.

I called Renee and she met me at the house, we inspected Ted's side of the bed and found what appeared to be dead lice. We then went to the guest room where he had been spending most nights because he, "couldn't sleep", we pulled back the sheet and found a battlefield of dead crabs.

"That son of a bitch!" fumed Renee, "He knew! He had to know!"

It all made sense now, his insistence on doing his own laundry, his lack of concern over my health scare, his attempt to distract me with talk of a waterfront home—Ted knew all along that he had crabs and he could care less that he had given them to me. A trip to the library and a little research told me everything I needed to know about contracting crabs, there was only one way to spread them from one person to another and it had nothing to do with bed sheets or toilet seats as he claimed.

* * * *

I no longer allowed Ted to sleep in my bed, he was banished to the guest room until I could figure out what to do. I no longer wanted to be married to him and I wanted nothing to do with the house.

Several weeks went by and I discovered that Ted had been sneaking out at night through the unalarmed window in the guest room, the mystery of the bent blinds was solved as I realized he'd likely been doing it for quite some time. The question was, why? I wondered if perhaps he was meeting someone.

I recalled an incident when he returned from a late night walk, short of breath, drenched in sweat and peering over his shoulder as if he were being followed. He conjured up a story that he had been threatened by a group of kids in a car.

"I'm sure they're harmless," I said at the time, now I wondered if perhaps they were chasing Ted for other reasons. His navy track suit made him almost invisible in the dark of night. Was he looking in windows? Was I living with a Peeping Tom? The thought of it made my skin crawl.

I went down to the police station and asked Sergeant Smith to check into Ted's background, I told her all about his strange behavior and while she couldn't find anything on record, she told me that meant nothing, "It could be he just hasn't been caught," she said.

The next day, Detective Bruce reminded me of the upcoming Medal of Valor Ceremony. Detective Jones had gone ahead and nominated me for the award and even though I had been reluctant to attend, I was grateful for the distraction from Ted and what I now considered, a failing marriage.

The night of the awards ceremony, I told Ted I didn't want him to attend. Instead I was flanked by my children and several close friends, all thrilled to take part in honoring me. I was hurt that my parents, sister and brother-in-law chose not to attend. There excuse was flimsy, but I was intent on focusing on those who supported and cared about me.

Ted insisted he be allowed to attend, but I remained adamant.

"No, this is something that happened before I met you and I only want those who helped me through it to be present," I said.

"How's it going to look if your husband isn't there," he asked.

"I don't care how it looks, everyone knows we're on the verge of a divorce," I said. My words were stinging, but they served in closing the subject.

The invitation to the ceremony listed the guidelines for being eligible for the award:

Extraordinary bravery...above and beyond the call of duty...risk of life

An act of heroism...outstanding service...extreme tenacity and devotion to duty

I felt a fleeting sense of pride in the fact that I qualified for such a prestigious award. A part of me felt unworthy of the attention, I wanted to recognize my children and those who stood by me during those difficult days. I found it hard to believe that nearly a year had gone by since the attack. I wrote thank you notes to Jeffery, Michelle and Lily and planned to present them at the ceremony.

At least three hundred people attended the event; local dignitaries, police officers and even the Mayor of Edmonds made an effort to be there. Senator Gary Nelson from Edmonds came over to shake my hand, he asked if I'd be interested in addressing the House of Representatives in Olympia, Washington on the importance of the rights of gun owners. I promised to think about it, he gave me his card and told me to call him if I ever needed anything.

I kept my eye on the door throughout the meal, I was afraid Ted would show up and ruin the entire evening. I silently swore to have him escorted out should he dare to make an appearance.

Touching cards and sentiments from friends and people in the community were plentiful and I was beginning to doubt I could get through the evening without breaking down. I realized I had come a long way since the attack, while Ted was a bump in the road to recovery, I had made progress and once I began to accept that fact, I realized Ted had no place in the life I longed to reclaim.

When the Certificates of Commendation were handed out, I took the opportunity to dole out my cards to my children,

Jeffery and Lily, how proud I am of both of you for your strength and knowledge which helped guide me...

And to Michelle,

Michelle, I will never forget how you held my hand and took care of me through the trauma of what had happened and how you protected me through the aftermath that followed...

When it came my turn, Major General Barlow stood beside me as Sheriff Scharf began reading my citation:

"During late 1992 and early 1993, a series of major assaults were carried out against women in the Edmonds/Lynnwood area..."

I could feel myself losing the battle for composure. Major General Barlow placed his arm around my shoulder to steady me. I turned away from the audience, I just didn't want to be seen—I didn't want to be there. I was grateful when the Sheriff concluded his speech,

"For the courage and fortitude to resist a dangerous, life-threatening attack, and her ability to fight back and apprehend the suspect, Ms. Morehouse is awarded a Medal of Merit."

The entire room broke into thunderous applause as Major General Barlow presented the framed medal. I cried at the outpouring of compassion and gratitude I was receiving from the crowd. Sheriff Scharf stepped to me, extended his hand and thanked me as he handed me the framed citation.

I saw out of the corner of my eye as Detective Jones stepped toward me, I buried my head in his chest and sobbed. He held me until I was able to regain my composure. Jeffery, Lily and Michelle beamed as people approached to shake my hand. Somehow, it felt like I had emerged from a very dark tunnel that I had spent the last year in. The display of human kindness helped me to understand that the world was made up of mostly good, and although the bad guys wield their wrath, in the end, kindness wins and justice is served.

My heart was warmed as we continued the celebration over cocktails with Detective Jones and his wife. Feeling a bit like Cinderella, I suggested I get home before midnight, it had been an emotionally draining experience, but I somehow felt I would sleep well that night.

* * * *

"Where the hell have you been?" Ted demanded. He met me at the door when I arrived home shortly after midnight.

"Relax, Ted. I was at the award ceremony," I was determined not to engage in an argument right before bed, I wouldn't have him ruin my night. I laid my framed award and the citation on the kitchen counter and bent down to fill Chanel's nearly empty water dish.

"That was over at ten-thirty!" he snapped.

I took a step back, How did he know? I watched as he reached for the frames, a sudden calm came over him and he smiled a sly smile, "I was so proud of you. It broke my heart to see you break down up there."

I was speechless, He was there! He was watching me!

I scooped up Chanel, "I'm going to bed," I said, trying hard to keep my composure. My stomach lurched as I realized what had happened, "I'm exhausted."

Without waiting for a response, I headed to my room, locked the door and pulled my gun from my purse and set it on the bedside table. My mind raced as I wondered what else this man was capable of. I knew I needed to escape this prison I had put myself in.

Within two days I arranged for my children and a few friends to help me move back to Kim and Renee's. We packed hastily and loaded a rented truck in a mere three hours. I videotaped the house so that I would have proof that it was in good condition when I left. I didn't want his tendency for trickery to end up framing me in spite.

I placed my house key on the kitchen counter and we left.

I never looked back.

CHAPTER 23 – BUSINESS—NOT AS USUAL

"Betrayal is common for men with no conscience."
~Toba Beta

I quickly filed for divorce from Ted and even though he continued to leave notes at the café, begging me to reconsider, his efforts were ignored and his final note was a simple, handwritten, "Goodbye" taped to the door.

I felt empowered that I was able to stand strong against his attempts at further manipulation and control. They had been too much for me when I was initially recovering from the attack, I was so intent on finding my way back that any path would do. Even an unhealthy one.

But things were different now and I was determined to continue my journey to a full recovery without Ted and his sick tactics. Jeffery and Michelle were relieved that I had moved on and Dr. Jantz encouraged me to remain on guard. He advised me to have someone accompany me whenever possible and Renee proved to be a strong-force in ensuring I was rarely alone.

Jeffery and Lily became engaged, they would be getting married in June and moving to Japan in August for the next two years. I was thrilled for them, even though I knew how much I would miss them. When they told me their news, I was surprised at my lack of panic. To be without them only a year earlier would have been unthinkable, and here I was wishing them well and willing them on to a bright and happy future together. They weren't the only ones embarking on a new beginning.

Sinus infections had been plaguing me since Chesnutt had stomped on my face, closing the two main sinus tracks. Thirteen months later I had surgery to re-open the tracks and stop the infections which served as nothing more than a painful reminder of Chesnutt's impact on my physical being.

I continued to test negative on HIV tests, but I continued to feel fatigue much of the time. I had trouble sleeping and wasn't sure if I should write it off to shifting hormones or to the fact that I still didn't feel completely in control of my own life. Dr. Newton put me back on anti-depressants.

* * * *

Laura, an employee whom I had hired shortly after the attack, had twice expressed interest in buying the café. I was spending less and less time at the business and she saw my lack of physical presence as a sign of waning interest in its future.

While it was true that I wasn't as present as I had been previously, I was intent on making sure the business was in good hands and that I would reap the rewards of the years I had invested in the café.

"I'll sell it to you for $70,000," I said. "That's well below market price." Laura said she'd speak to her boyfriend and get back to me.

Laura called to say she and her boyfriend were very interested, he would either borrow the money or sell some stocks to pay for the business. They knew they were getting a good deal and didn't plan to let it slip away.

They began to push me to handle the incidentals of the sale, but to be honest, I was overwhelmed. Lily and Jeffery's wedding, my impending divorce and a move that would seal the deal that I would not be returning to the house that Ted and I had shared. I leased a home in Edmonds and was in the process of moving my belongings there. Poor Chanel had become so accustomed to staying in different homes, she adapted well to wherever we went. I was constantly on guard, watching for Ted in my rearview mirror.

I didn't like being alone at night, but I found it safer than being with Ted. I'd keep the TV on as long as I could, I'd wait until I was so tired that it didn't matter that someone might enter my room and kill me. Somehow, I'd find sleep, or sleep would find me. I was always grateful to wake to the light of day.

One day one of my regular customers asked if I was, "...working for the new owner." When I told her I was still the owner she said she'd been told that I had sold the business to Laura. I realized in her over-zealous enthusiasm to buy the café, Laura was telling customers the sale had already occurred. I began to feel more and more detached from the business and decided to just get the sale over with.

I soon found out that the decision wouldn't be mine. In order to sell the business to Laura and her boyfriend, I'd have to ensure they had a three to five-year lease on the property where the business was located. I understood their desire for guaranteed amount of time to recoup their investment, but when I contacted my landlord he told me he had just recently been made an offer on the property and was seriously considering selling.

I was surprised, "You said you'd never sell the property," I said. He'd always been more than fair with me, and I had nothing in writing to say he would never sell, but I took him at his word.

"It's an offer that's just too good to pass up," he said. He lived in Alaska and I could understand his own desire to free himself from ownership and possibly walk away with a nice bundle of cash in the process.

I told Laura that I couldn't guarantee the lease and she and her boyfriend became furious.

"We spent over three-thousand dollars on attorney fees!" he snapped.

"I never told you to have papers drawn," I said. "Perhaps you should have waited until we ironed out the details."

A few days later my landlord called to tell me the offer for the property had stalled and asked if I'd like to purchase it outright for $275,000.00. That was a lot of money for me and I was reluctant to make such a major decision without giving it a lot of thought and research. If I purchased the property which consisted of the building I currently leased for the café, along with a 10,000 square foot warehouse with poor wiring and no heat. I knew an automotive repair shop had been there years before, and discovered that I could probably rent it for close to $2,000 a month "as is", and pass the cost of any upgrades on to my leaser.

Upon telling Laura and her boyfriend that I was considering buying the property and could then sell them the café and allow them to pay rent to me, they were thrilled. My landlord gave me a month to secure the loan, but I was to discover that there was far more involved. I had to submit plans to the City of Edmonds of what was to be done with the property, notify local property owners of my intent and allow them to challenge the sale. I learned the process could take upwards of six months—that was time I didn't have.

I remembered Senator Nelson's words to me at the Medal of Valor Ceremony, "If I can ever do anything to help you, please don't hesitate to call." I decided that this would be a perfect time to cash in that chip and I made a call to him.

"I'll be glad to see what I can do to speed things up," he said.

Two days later I met with the City of Edmonds Planning Department and the engineer said, "I think we can hurry this along for you and get it pushed through if you can compile a list of all local businesses.

Beth, a close friend of Kim's was recovering from knee surgery and offered to help during her convalescence, "I'm dying for something to do," she said. I was grateful as it looked as though my friends and contacts in high places would help me in saving my business. The next step was to apply for a loan to purchase the property.

A customer of mine called and told me he had been in the Snohomish County Administration building and had spotted Laura and her boyfriend speaking to an engineer.

"She said she knew the property Caffé Aida is on was for sale and wanted to know how they could purchase it and how much notice they would need to give you to vacate the property. It sounded like they're planning to open their own coffee shop."

I nearly fell off my chair, after all I had done for Laura, she was planning to betray me and run me out of business. This knife in my back hurt almost as much as Chesnutt's and I couldn't help but feel

I was once again the victim. "How could she be so devious?" I thought.

If they succeeded in buying the property, they could simply kick me off and start their own coffee business and, in essence, steal my customers and conjure up any story they liked. Laura continued to be her own sweet self to me, with never a mention of their intention to double-cross me. I didn't let on that I was aware of their plans, but I could barely look at her when we were at the café. I didn't have the time, nor the energy, to train a new employee. This latest assault on my trust took me three steps backward in my recovery. I felt exhausted when faced with the idea of confronting Laura and her boyfriend. The feeling was reminiscent of my first days after Chesnutt's attack.

I decided not to say anything to Laura, I'd go ahead and proceed with purchasing the property myself. Strange things continued to happen, obscene phone calls in the middle of the night disrupted my sleep and made me sure that Ted had somehow found my number. A late night knock at the door by a couple of college boys fueled my paranoia that they were not looking for a party, as they said they were, but were out to get me.

My deadline to secure financing on the property was quickly approaching and I was having difficulty focusing on the task of compiling all the necessary information to seek approval of the loan. Beth continued to help me, but I was once again immersed in the fog that accompanies an attack. Laura's threat to my business made me uneasy and had me constantly looking over my shoulder in a desperate attempt to win the race for approval to purchase the property and save the café. Why I didn't just outright fire her, I can't answer. I felt paralyzed to act on the silent assault that was going on behind my back. It seemed easier to "wait it out" than to get into a territorial battle with her. In the end, I hoped that good would prevail.

A visit from the county health department would inform me that the household refrigerators in my storage shed were not up to code. I was asked to either upgrade to expensive commercial refrigerators or cease in using the household refrigerators I had purchased after the attack. I simply could not carry the crates of milk needed for the everyday demands of a trendy coffee business due to the injuries I had sustained from Chesnutt, but at more than $6,000 for two commercial refrigerators, an absolutely unaffordable expense, I would have to figure out a plan B—which would have me revert to picking up heavy crates from the local dairy and lifting them into my car. I wondered how the health department had become aware of my refrigerators in the first place.

Time was running out and I was informed by the bank that I had been denied the loan. My outline for a financial plan for the property with more than 50% of the property intended to sublet was not in compliance with their requirements for a secure loan and so, I was denied.

The property was sold to a couple who planned to tear down the warehouse and build an orthodontic office. Laura inquired as to what I had planned for the business and I told her, "Nothing." I was intent on denying her any ammunition to hurt me or the business any further. In time, I would call and advise her that I wouldn't be needing her services anymore.

I told her how surprised I was that she and her boyfriend had been looking into purchasing the property and had plans to kick me off. She denied it until I told her how I had been given the information; where they were, who they were speaking with and what was said. She became angry and hung up on me. Her boyfriend called back and attempted to smooth things over.

"I know what you were up to and I don't appreciate the dishonesty, I've always been more than honest with Laura. I would have appreciated if you would have granted me the same courtesy." That would be the last time I spoke with either of them.

I learned sometime later that she would lose other jobs due to dishonesty and substance abuse.

* * * *

Things continued to be peculiar at the café, employees were stealing from me and they had clever ways of doing it. One of the ways I was able to track sales was to count cups and monitor the coffee bean containers. A sleeve of one-hundred cups was equal to an average of $400 in sales. I was suspicious that sales seemed way down and while the cup inventory was high, the bean inventory continued to diminish, so I installed a surveillance camera.

An employee was caught on tape bringing in a sleeve of cups—the very same that the café used—during her shift. She'd use her own cup, pretend to ring up the sale and pocket the money. When I called her to let her know I'd no longer be using her services, she replied with, "You fucking bitch!" and hung up on me. I never had to tell her that I had finally caught her, or how.

She wasn't the only one, they pocketed cash out of the money bag which was used to stock the cash drawer for change, telling me I had forgotten to put the money in. They counted on me being forgetful and spacy. It still happened from time to time, I'd be in the middle of a sentence and simply forget what I was about to say. It was frustrating and I'm sure I came across as an easy target by some of these girls and women.

They stopped wearing their required uniforms, they were late to work and didn't bother to do inventory correctly.

On a particular morning, I went in for a shift change and the employee who opened told me she wasn't feeling well. I was well aware of her history of drug and alcohol abuse.

"Are you on drugs?" I asked. She responded with an uncontrollable laugh, "No, but a few of my girlfriends and I went out drinking last night," she said. She could hardly stand up and I told her to go home for a few hours to sleep it off. I was angry that she had been representing the café in front of customers before I got there, I could only imagine how she had appeared to them.

When she didn't return several hours late I went to her apartment. My knocks at her door went unanswered and I finally managed to get the landlord to let me in. There she lay in the middle of the living room floor. I thought she was dead, but she moved her head, mumbled something unintelligible and passed out again.

"Get up!" I yelled, "I'm taking you to the hospital!"

This girl had been late so many times, and now this. I knew I needed to fire her, but I didn't have the energy. Renee offered to do the deed for me, I knew in my heart of hearts that before the attack I would not have put up with the behavior I was now allowing to sabotage my business. I had no energy to stand up to them—I had lost control.

One by one, I managed to catch the culprits in the act of stealing and eventually Renee and I drafted a procedural manual that would be a mandatory tool requiring operating steps that would make employee theft difficult to impossible. I spent more time at the café training old staff that had been loyal as well as new staff.

One of my new employees was Mike's daughter, Gina, I knew she would never steal from me and hired her on the spot when she came in looking for a job. This brought Mike back into my life and we started dating again, he was once again on the verge of divorce and we actually became a nice distraction to one another; me from the chaos of a business on the brink of failure, and him from the chaos of a marriage on the brink of failure.

He called often and we enjoyed dinners together, he stayed with me for several weeks before getting his own place. We were more like very good friends, rather than romantic lovers. He had given up his contracting business in order to buy a deli with his, now estranged, wife and found the restaurant business wasn't for him. He wanted to re-establish his contracting business and he knew that meant starting from scratch. I encouraged him to follow his passion.

I mustered up my determination to find a new place for the café. The new landlords had plans to raise my rent by 600%. That was out of the question for a small espresso business.

One day I happened to be in the bowling alley and the owner said he'd heard I was looking for new space and asked if I'd consider moving to his parking lot. I was excited at the prospect and although there was much in the way of logistics and red tape to discover if it would all work, I was once again hopeful.

On March 24, 1995, Michelle delivered a baby boy. He would be named Evan Thomas and he would let me know that the world could still be a beautiful place.

I was instantly in love.

CHAPTER 24 – GOODBYE MIKE, HELLO BRAD

"If you're brave enough to say goodbye, life will reward you with a new hello."

~Paulo Coelho

It wasn't my intention, but Mike and I drifted apart. He was busy with divorce proceedings, trying to detach from the deli and rebuild his contracting business. We touched base by phone every few weeks, but the dinner dates ceased and I was now immersed in my new role of grandmother. We seemed to weave in and out of one another's lives just when we needed it most, I'd like to think I helped him as much as he helped me navigate the good and the bad.

Evan was adorable and both Tom and I were thrilled to be grandparents. Michelle slipped easily into motherhood, although I often worried that she hadn't fully dealt with the attack on her own mother, Evan seemed to bring out a calmer, gentler side of her that I hoped would still the waters of anger and fear that came with knowing the bad guys did exist and they could easily alter lives in an instant.

I drove the hour from my home to Michelle's and Jake's at least twice a week to see and play with Evan. When I wasn't with him, I was thinking of him and planning my next trip.

I had yet to secure a new place for the café, but this time the red tape of local government was on my side. The new owner of the property contacted me to advise that glitches with the City of Edmonds' requirements for the dental clinic they planned to construct would cause them to delay breaking ground for several more months. This would allow me more time to find a new location with far less urgency.

Having rid myself of the sticky-fingered employees, I was taking more shifts at the café. One afternoon a utility crew was working several feet from the café, they were close enough that I could see them eying me as I served my customers. If I glanced over, I was met with a smile.

As I prepared to leave the café to pick up supplies, one of the workers approached me, "Hi," he said, "are you married or going with someone?"

I was completely taken aback, "No, I'm not," I said, not completely sure I should have said anything at all, but he seemed nice and not threatening in the least. He was attractive with a kind face and a smile in his voice.

"Good," he continued, "can I take you to dinner sometime?"

I surprised myself when I said, "Sure." He told me his name was Aiden and I gave him my phone number. I left the lot and returned a little while later to unload. As I was stocking the supplies another utility worker drove to the window, he wore sunglasses and had a big, dazzling smile. I found him even more attractive than Aiden. I was disappointed I hadn't met him before Aiden had approached me. His name was Brad and he and Aiden were friends, I supposed he knew that Aiden had asked me to dinner and I wondered if there was a friendly competition for my attention in the works.

Aiden phoned that very evening and we talked for more than an hour. We made arrangements to have dinner the next evening after my shift.

He picked me up at my home and we went to dinner, while it was nice, I felt no spark. He continued to call, but I consistently made up excuses why I couldn't go out, hoping he'd become disinterested and stop calling. I didn't want to hurt his feelings, but the truth was that I just wasn't attracted to him.

Finally, after several weeks of an occasional meal here and there and many more declines on my part, he said, "You always seem so busy."

"You're a very nice man," I said, "but I'm really not interested in dating anyone right now. I have so much going on; I really don't have the time." He was gracious as I let him down easy, but he seemed to get my message as he didn't call after that.

Brad continued his daily ritual of iced mochas, telling me I made the best in town. One day he lingered a little longer than usual.

"You do realize I only stop when you're here," he said. "I look for your car," his smile was shy and sweet and I felt something stir inside and realized I was smiling right back at him.

We talked for a while, I learned he had recently broken up with his girlfriend, "She's an alcoholic," he said. "I never should have started dating her, she's a customer service rep at the same company, but was recently transferred to another building, so I don't really run into her anymore."

The brief visits continued and I'd discover more about Brad with each one. He was divorced a few years earlier and had two children, ages five and eight. The marriage ended when he learned of his ex-wife's affair, "That's the deal-breaker for me, there's no going back after that." That was exactly how I'd felt about Tom's infidelity and I was glad we shared a common view on the importance of being faithful.

After nearly two months of treading cautiously, Brad asked me out.

"Can you meet me for a drink later?" I hated to turn him down, but I was to attend the City of Edmonds hearing that evening to determine if I would be allowed to relocate the café to the bowling alley lot. There was an Albertson's supermarket in the same shopping center and the fear was that my business would infringe on parking for their customers.

Brad understood the importance of my being at the hearing and told me he was leaving the next morning to spend the weekend in Montana with his mother, but promised we'd go out as soon as he returned. He gave me his cell phone number and asked me to call him when I was home from the hearing.

After a short presentation, the City of Edmonds voted to allow me to relocate my business. I was thrilled that after all the ups and downs of not knowing if my business could survive the new owners of my current location, I still had a future with the café. I would just need to begin informing my customers of my new location.

I called Brad with the good news and he said he was at a local restaurant with a friend and asked if I could meet him there. He was waiting for me in the lounge when I arrived.

"I'm so glad we're finally able to get together," he said. The next two hours flew by as we shared stories, laughed and learned more about one another. It felt a little like a school-girl crush, complete with butterflies and the anticipation of when we'd be able to see one another again.

The next morning Brad surprised me by showing up at the café, "I couldn't leave without seeing you one more time," he said. "I'd like to see you Sunday night, I'll be home back in town before dark." He leaned down and kissed me, to my surprise.

"I'll be thinking of you the whole time I'm gone," he said.

My school-girl crush was now a full-grown woman, full on romance, "I'll be here," I said.

For the first time in a long time, I meant it.

* * * *

Two weeks into our dating Brad told me he wanted us to be exclusive, "I have no intention of dating anyone else," he confided. His voice was low and seductive as he spoke into my ear.

"Neither do I," I said. For the first time since Tom, I felt my heart flutter; my desire for him was real and undeniable.

He gave me a key to his home and asked that I be there each evening, as soon as I could. Most nights I'd stay with him, grateful for his protective arms, I slept so well. Until the phone rang.

Linda called often. Brad would answer the phone and yell into the receiver, "Stop calling me, it's over!" He'd hang up and tell me it was Linda and she was drunk.

Nearly every night I'd stay with him the ritual continued, I'd fall asleep, only to be awakened by the phone and Brad yelling into the receiver, "Don't call here! I'm seeing someone else!" and hang up. But the damage would be done, once woken, I found it terribly hard to fall back to sleep.

Until the night he gave me one of his Zanex. I slept soundly and longer than I had since the attack. I couldn't remember a deeper, more gratifying sleep and I wanted more, so my date with Zanex became a nightly ritual. I could barely remember the phone ringing in the dead of night, if it jarred me for a moment, I'd quickly fall back into deep sleep. It became a welcome escape.

The phone rang during dinner one night and Brand hung up on Linda once more, "Why does she keep calling?" I asked. I was finding her intrusions to be more and more aggravating.

"She's still in love with me," he said. I was bewildered at her insistence on being a part of his life when it was clear he had moved on.

We had been dating about three months when Brad asked me about my ex-boyfriends.

"Has anyone called you lately?" he asked. He was suddenly curious about my daily plans; who was I seeing—where was I going. I could tell by his questions that he didn't trust me.

I would return his calls as soon as possible and was always met with questions of, "Where are you?" and, "Who are you with?" followed by, "How long will you be there?" I had never given him any reason to mistrust me and I reasoned that his ex-wife's affair might have stirred his paranoia. I concluded that if Linda would leave us alone and Brad could learn to trust again, then we would have a perfect relationship.

One night after making love, Brad confessed his love to me, "I love you," he said.

"I love you, too." I stated, "You and your children and your entire family." He smiled and pulled me close. I was certain I had found my forever place in his arms.

* * * *

Dr. Jantz suggested I pay my utility bill in person, "Ask her how her relationship with Brad is going." I was shocked at his suggestion.

"It's over," I insisted, "he's not seeing her anymore."

"If that's true then it shouldn't be a big deal. You shouldn't be afraid of the truth." It was as if he knew something I didn't and I was determined to prove him wrong, but his words resonated with me, "The truth doesn't hurt."

Beth drove me to the utility company and stayed in the car as I went in to pay my bill. I knew what Linda looked like thanks to a picture Brad had shown me from the company handbook. I took a deep breath and went inside.

Linda was on the telephone when I entered, I waited until she hung up and approached,

"Hi, do you have a minute?" She seemed to know who I was and her eyes welled with tears.

"Yes," she said.

"How's it going with Brad," I asked. Her response threw me.

"Not very good," she answered.

"When was the last time you spoke with him?" I was well aware her words might sting, but I was determined to find out the truth.

"I saw him at lunch, today." My insides froze as I delved deeper, "Where?" I asked.

"His house," she said.

I couldn't believe what I was hearing. "You do know that Brad and I have been seeing one another," I said, as if my verbal claim to him would change anything.

"Have you been seeing him since I've been seeing him?" My hunger for the truth seemed almost masochistic.

"We've been having sex three or four times a week," she confessed. I was stunned. Once again I was handed the role of victim.

"When did this start?" I asked.

196

"It never stopped," she answered.

She went on to tell me that on the nights I would go home, he would call her and ask her to come over. She would spend the night and leave for work from his house.

I was stunned, but not necessarily surprised. It was odd, but I almost expected her answers to the mysteries Brad presented.

"Can we get a drink?" she asked, "I'm off in a few minutes," she said. I told her I could, but I would need a ride home. She told me she'd take me home and I stepped outside and let Beth know I would be okay and thanked her.

"He's sleeping with the former girlfriend," I said. Beth's mouth dropped, "Oh, my God!" she managed. Her face mirrored my feelings—I'd become the victim once more.

I found the role tiresome.

* * * *

I confronted Brad and his reaction was text-book, he instantly shot back that I shouldn't have been snooping behind his back.

"I need some time," I said. I wanted to be alone to think about where my life had been and where it was headed. With two failed marriages under my belt and the threat of a third if I decided to spend my life with a philanderer, I had to have some quiet hours to determine what my next steps would be.

We kept in touch and the contact would eventually lead me back to Brad's bed. One night he asked, "Have you spoken to Linda?" I found the question odd, Linda and I were not friends, in fact, our only common thread was Brad.

"You two were such good friends," he insisted. "I was just wondering if you've spoken."

"We're not friends," I said. "My friends would never sleep with someone I was sleeping with."

Brad dropped the subject.

I wondered why Brad was so concerned with whether I had spoken to Linda, I decided to call her.

"Linda, it's Maddie. Have you spoken to Brad?"

"He called me yesterday," she said. "He said you two broke up."

"Oh, really?" I said, "I spent the night at his house last night. He's lying again!" There was an incredible force that rose in me, "I think we need to confront him!"

Instead of being beaten down by the actions of others, I was oddly empowered to fight for what I knew was right. I was tired of the wrong, tired of being victim to the disloyalty and foolery of those in which I placed my trust.

I couldn't wait to surprise Brad.

CHAPTER 25 – THE ART OF DISCARDING

"Moving on is easy. It's staying moved on that's trickier."
~Katerina Stoykova Klemer

Brad's mother, sister and brother-in-law were returning from Germany the following evening and I insisted on accompanying him to pick them up from the airport. I instructed Linda that I would call her when we returned to Brad's and his family had left for home. At that point, she would just show up at Brad's and the confrontation would begin.

On the ride from the airport, Brad's family was tired and sitting in the backseat, they told us a little of their trip to Germany, but mostly they wanted to rest. Brad leaned into me and asked, "When was the last time you spoke to Linda?"

I couldn't help but smile at my firm grasp of the upper hand, "Today," I answered. "In fact she's coming over tonight."

Brad stiffened and took my hand. We bid his family goodnight in the driveway and they left for their own homes. We went inside and Brad ushered his kids off to bed, "Did you say you invited Linda here?" he asked.

"Yes," I said. "She's waiting for my call."

"Why would you do that?" he was suddenly a bundle of nerves.
"You'll see," was my only reply.

I called Linda and told her we were home; within minutes the doorbell rang. "You invited her here, you let her in," Brad said.

I opened the door for Linda, she entered and went straight to the back porch to smoke. Brad hated the smell of cigarette smoke and refused to allow it in the house, it was clear Linda knew his rule and honored it.

"Can I get you a drink?" I asked when she came back inside.

"Vodka—with orange juice," she said, she then sat down across from Brad. The awkward silence was deafening until I placed her drink in front of her, it seemed to provide her with a voice.

"You're quite a shit," she said. Brad sat in silence, like a child who had been caught with his hands in the cookie jar.

"You can't have it both ways," I said as I sat down at the table. "You have to make a decision," his silence spoke volumes, the man was pushed to the wall.

He looked at Linda, "You know I love Maddie," he said. "I know I've hurt her and I hope she'll forgive me." Linda gulped her drink in disgust, "You're the one who called me, Brad."

"I won't call you anymore," he said. "I love Maddie."

Linda rose from her chair and bent down to kiss Brad on the lips. He showed no emotion and when she walked out the door, he looked at me and asked, "Are you happy now?"

"Am I happy that you called her again? No!" My reply was directed at myself as much as it was Brad.

We went to bed and my lover that night would be three Zanex lulling me into precious sleep.

* * * *

Our relationship continued to be a roller coaster, I showed up to do chores around Brad's house and when I would go home for a few days, he'd call telling me how much he missed me. Linda was a constant topic in our conversations, often leading to arguments.

"You will never trust me, will you?" he'd ask.

"You're the one calling her!" I'd respond. I instinctively knew their relationship was a hotbed for our own and while I was willing to fight for Brad, I felt their history was stronger than my will.

I stuck around, I cooked and cleaned and made sure Brad's children were looked after when they were at his home, but my world was about to widen.

One morning while I was paying bills at my house in Edmonds, the phone rang. It was a new television show called Day & Date.

The producer of the show had read an article about me and wanted to know if I was willing to be interviewed. I decided to do the interview, I had somehow grown stronger and was ready to share my story.

I'm not certain what had changed; less than a year earlier I had insisted it was my twin that was raped and lauded a local hero for capturing the man who had terrorized women in a small Washington town. I was reluctant to divulge my own address, I wasn't quite ready to go that far, so Brad said it would be okay if the interview was conducted at his house and we set up a date and time.

The afternoon of the interview the crew arrived and parked a satellite truck in Brad's driveway. The reporter, Dana, coached me on how we'd proceed.

"We'll start with the 911 tape," she said, "but we can block the audio feed to your headset, if you'd prefer."

"I think that might be best," I said. The feed would be carried live and I wasn't sure how I'd react to the traumatic recording, I didn't want to embarrass myself by possibly breaking down.

Dana began the interview by asking about my history as a rape counselor. A pang of guilt hit me as I thought of Cassie Haden and the fact that we never did meet again. My own attack would overshadow hers.

"Do you think your experience as a counselor helped you in dealing with your own attack?" Dana asked.

"I don't think anything can prepare you for a violent crime," I said. "One shouldn't be expected to 'deal' with it on their own, I'm a firm believer in counseling and I still see a local counselor, Dr. Greg Jantz."

When the interview was over, I was glad I had done it. If nothing else, maybe my endorsement for counseling would help others who had suffered a similar fate. Hiding away, tucking the experience into the back of a closet along with Valor plaques that only served to remind me that, locked away or not, Chesnutt still walked this earth, hadn't really gotten me past the emotional pain of being the victim.

Claiming the ordeal happened to a twin that didn't exist and tumbling headlong into unhealthy relationships hadn't brought me to a better place. Aside from receiving the Medal of Merit, the interview seemed to be a first step in discarding the cloak that hid my new identity. I was exposed to a national audience of women whose greatest fear was likely the very thing I had lived to tell about and men who struggled to understand how to help their sisters, wives or girlfriends who had been victims themselves, reclaim their lives.

Something about that was empowering.

* * * *

Brad and I continued an on again, off again relationship. Things would be fine and he'd suddenly start an argument, saying hurtful things that would give me no other choice but to leave and let him cool off. After one of those episodes I found myself missing him and was determined to get to the bottom of his unpredictable behavior.

I got in my car and drove to his house only to find Linda's car in the driveway. I didn't stop. The next morning, I confronted him and his response was to tell me he liked me better the way I was when I first met him. This person who could stick up for herself was more than he wanted to deal with.

I took a moment to recall who I was when Brad and I met; an injured bird, coming off of a disastrous marriage and still trying to heal from a catastrophic event. That's how he preferred me. It was important that I understood that fact, but habits die hard and it would take me a little longer to brave a clean break.

* * * *

The relocation of the café was imminent, the owners of the property were set to break ground for the dental clinic and my days of reasonable rent were numbered. I had been told by the owners of the bowling alley that they looked forward to having me in their lot and my last step was to get the final signatures from the regional manager of Albertson's. My café would take up five of their parking spots; five spots that I had been eying and knew were almost never used by either Albertson customers, or visitors to the bowling alley.

The regional manager was less than approachable, "I wasn't told anything about this," he said.

"It's been in the works for months," I countered. "There's a Starbucks across the street at one of your biggest competitors. This could be good for business, I have a good customer base, they'll buy a cup of coffee and figure they might as well pick up a few grocery items while they're here. How can that not be good for everyone?" I smiled, desperate to win over this sour man who probably hated his job, his life, the world.

"Please," I said, "my customers are expecting me here Monday morning. I don't want to disappoint them."

"I'm sorry, Ms. Morehouse," his delivery told me he wasn't sorry at all. "You should have gone through the proper channels, all items concerning the use of Albertson property in this region need my approval. I'm afraid I can't approve this."

I was devastated. I was about to lose my business, the business I had worked so hard to build; the business that had likely saved me as it served as a distraction and a necessity during my recovery. Brad had accompanied me to the meeting and as we left Albertson's, he put his arm around me and pulled me close as I cried. It was those moments I was grateful he was still a constant in my life, but they were becoming less and less frequent.

That weekend we dismantled my café equipment and with much help, moved the building to the beautiful property of a dear friend. My business was in pieces. Put away with no plans to serve customers in search of mochas on a Monday—or any other day. In fact, Caffé Aida would never reopen. I was reluctant to abandon the business I had grown to love, but the next several months would help me to understand why I needed to be free of the paperwork, the inventory, the day-to-day activity of meeting, greeting and pouring for customers...

just people in search of a cup of coffee and a smile.

* * * *

I let my landlord know I'd be moving—yet again. Like my darling Puka, my hard-earned café, another failed marriage and my best friend having had recently died of cancer, it was time to let go of something I relied on to see me to someplace better—my home.

Brad asked me to move in with him and I declined, instead taking Tom's sister up on her offer to rent a spare room. Mary Jane said I was welcome to it, for as long as needed. I felt that my decision to turn Brad down was a positive, I was ready to brave it alone, once more.

One thing that could not be discarded was the love and generosity of the Morehouse family and friends.

CHAPTER 26 – THREE STEPS BACK

"I found myself in a sea in which the waves of joy and sorrow were clashing against each other."

~Naguib Mahfouz

My cellphone rang early one morning, "Hello? Ms. Morehouse?"

"This is she," I said in the same hurried tone I reserved for telemarketers, determined to make the conversation short and sweet.

"I'm calling on behalf of the Montel Williams show," he said. "We'd like to tell your story."

They were doing a segment on people who had taken the law into their own hands and won in the process. Although I felt nothing like a winner, I agreed to do the show. They would fly me and a guest to New York City, put us up in a beautiful hotel and cart us by limo to and from the studio.

I had never been to New York and felt the experience was too good to pass up. With Jeffery still in Japan, I asked Michelle to accompany me. It took her less than fifteen minutes to re-arrange her plans and make arrangements for Evan to be cared for in her absence. She was on board with a resounding, "Yes!"

I let Brad know I'd be gone for a few days, we were still on-again-off-again at any moment, so I felt no real obligation. He was hurt that I hadn't asked him, but I had little in the way of empathy. My heart was wrapped up in spending time with my daughter and he'd have to wait his turn, as between his encounters with Linda, I had to wait mine.

My weakness for falling in and out of the relationship concerned me as I was well aware it wasn't exclusive, I wrote it off to the fact that I was still reluctant to be alone. While I wasn't comfortable with disloyalty, I knew deep down that when the sun set, I was more comfortable with another person, preferably a man, in the house. I suppose I was using Brad as much as he was using Linda and I. I also knew I would one day be strong enough to move on—just not yet.

When Michelle and I arrived in New York, a limousine was waiting to take us to our hotel in the heart of Manhattan. We quickly unpacked our luggage and headed out to explore the city. The trip, shopping and dinner left us both exhausted and grateful for the turned-down bed and fluffed pillows when we returned. Michelle was asleep before her head hit the pillow; per usual, I laid awake into the wee hours.

The following morning a limo picked us up and took us to the studio to tape the show. The hustle and bustle of the city was something I'd only read about in books and seen in movies. The movers and shakers hit the streets early, coffee and cell phones in hand, hurrying to their destinations, unaware of those in their path, just destined for their next meeting or power lunch. I wondered if I could keep up in such a fast-paced world, and decided I was a much better visitor than New York City native.

We arrived at the studio and the producer advised that they'd like to begin the show with my story. I panicked at the thought of being first and they juggled the line-up and said they'd put me last. Montel Williams came into the green room to meet Michelle and I, he was kind and personable and I instantly felt more relaxed.

Michelle was escorted to her seat during a commercial break and I was brought to the stage. I scanned the audience and found Michelle, she had tears running down her face and my impulse was to jump off stage and embrace her. The urge to do so was interrupted by Montel introducing me and the 911 call spilling from the sound system.

I knew the nature of the taped call, the desperation in my voice, my language and the sheer violence of it all was going to be too much for Michelle. Her face was tense as she dabbed at her eyes with a damp tissue. The tape finally ended with my words to my attacker, "How old are you going to be when you die?"

The audience applauded and the interview began. I recounted the entire ordeal of that fateful night and its aftermath; the overdose and how Michelle's quick thinking saved my life. Montel approached her and she stood, but she was just too overcome to answer any question. He placed his arm around her shoulder, "Why don't you join your mother on stage."

I watched as my brave and wonderful daughter made her way to me. It was reminiscent of when she was a little girl and had been hurt in some way; a bully on the playground, a skinned knee, a tumble off her two-wheeler. I instinctively rose to embrace her as my segment came to an end with a fade to commercial break. The show aired on January 19th, 1996.

We spent the next day taking in all the sights of the city. New York lived up to its reputation of bright lights, big city, complete with the movers, shakers and fashionistas who kept it alive, vibrant and exciting twenty-four hours a day.

We would return to Edmonds a little worldlier for the experience.

* * * *

I didn't recall a regular pattern of nightmares, but a particularly violent one, complete with screams and flailing arms, during an overnight stay at Brad's, had him wondering if the talk show circuit was such a great idea.

"It's conjuring up too much," he insisted the next morning over coffee. "By the way, when was the last time you checked with the Department of Corrections on his whereabouts?"

"They're not going to move him from Walla Walla," I said, "I'm sure he's still there."

"I'd check if I were you, they're not required to hunt you down and let you know when he's been moved. That's up to you," he took a last swig of coffee and left for work, leaving me with the nagging feeling that he was right.

By mid-morning I decided to calm my angst and confirm that Chesnutt was safely tucked away at Walla Walla Penitentiary for the next seventy-five years, he'd be a weak, rotted, feeble ninety-nine-year-old goat when he got out. Hardly capable of being a threat to anyone.

I called the department and gave the man Chesnutt's doc number.

I could hear as he punched the keys on his computer, "Allan Ray Chesnutt's been moved to Twin Rivers Correctional Facility in Monroe, Washington."

I felt my stomach lurch, I was overcome with fear, Monroe was a mere twenty minutes from me. "How can that be? He was given seventy-seven years, without the possibility of parole," I wanted him to tell me there had been a terrible mistake, I wanted him to thank me for pointing it out and assure me that they would get right on moving him back to Walla Walla, a somewhat safe distance of five hours away.

Instead he rattled off Chesnutt's counselor's name and phone number at Twin Rivers, "I suggest starting there," he said. My hand shook as I dialed the number, I was catapulted to three years before, to the days following the attack when I felt anything but safe.

My call was taken by a woman who would advise me that Twin Rivers was a minimum to medium security facility. I hung up and instantly called Dr. Jantz, his wife answered the phone and told me he was with a client.

"Please get him," I begged. "Chesnutt's in Monroe—he's right here." My breath came in short gasps and my chest was heaving like I'd just sprinted four blocks.

"Hold on, Maddie. Try and calm down," she put me on hold and I paced Brad's living room for what seemed like eternity. Finally, Dr. Jantz came to the phone, the sound of his voice was an instant relief. He told me to contact Chesnutt's counselor directly and get the information as to why he was transferred and what assurance I had that he would serve out his sentence.

Christina's voice was far more pleasant than the information she would give me, "Mr. Chesnutt was transferred to Twin Rivers for good behavior. But I can assure you he'll be spending a long time at Twin Rivers."

"I've been in my own prison for three years," I said. My voice was shaking and I was dangerously close to a deluge of hot tears.

"I'm sure you have," it was clear the call was going nowhere. While she was kind in her delivery, I was well aware I'd have to consider other avenues. I thought about his other victims, Did they know how close he was to us?

I grabbed the local phone directory and tried to look them up by last name, after several random phone calls, I could not find one of Chesnutt's victims to share the information I had. It occurred to me that they may have left Washington, or changed their phone numbers to unlisted; something I, myself, did. I could understand their determination to start a new life and never look back.

Maybe not such a bad idea.

* * * *

The next day I was scheduled to be interviewed by "Hard Copy", a syndicated show that focused on sensational news stories. The demand for my account of three years before was on the rise and seemed to score ratings, making me a commodity to these types of shows.

The interview lasted more than two hours, but in the back of my mind was the fact that the monster I was describing was just twenty minutes away. I was once again immersed in fog; any closure had been ripped away.

Two days later Brad and I attended a conference in Seattle for his work. Lovely dinners and a beautiful hotel suite should have been just the distraction I needed, but it would be there I learned from an attendee, Alex, who'd met us for cocktails and had served time at Twin Rivers years earlier, what purpose Twin Rivers really served.

We had left the lounge and continued our visit in our fifth floor suite when I asked Alex what Twin Rivers was like. His eyes shifted from me to Brad.

"You really want to know?" he asked. Brad nodded, "I think she needs to," he said.

Alex took a deep breath, "When you're transferred to Twin Rivers, you're being groomed for release." I gasped as he continued his description of prison accommodations that rivaled our hotel room.

"You're given a key to your room, so your privacy and belongings are protected. You have the ability to keep others out."

"Privacy!?" I was horrified, "Chesnutt doesn't deserve privacy!" I moved to the open window of our room and looked down to the pavement some five stories below. I pictured Chesnutt in his room, enjoying his new found path to freedom once more. Freedom to terrorize after just three short years of incarceration for ruining the lives of ten people. I thought of how I had lost my sense of self, my sense of security, my home and my business. I thought of how sleep was forever fleeting and that I couldn't fall into a deep satisfying slumber without the help of sleep aids.

Alex continued on about gym privileges, meals that put the local Denny's to shame and access to libraries. His voice faded in and out as I looked to the pavement below, I had always been afraid of heights, but suddenly I wasn't afraid. My head was completely wrapped around the "busted birds", as Tom's sister used to refer to the broken, the damaged, the emotionally impaired—Chesnutt had left behind ten busted birds and now it seemed he'd soon be free to bust even more.

Jump! Jump! Get it over with, just jump!

I leaned further out the window to my own freedom from the nightmare that had plagued me for three years now. Suddenly, Evan's face popped into my head. It was the sweet smile of my darling grandson that would cause me to step back into the room. I looked around and both Brad and Alex seemed oblivious to what I had almost done.

"Excuse me," I said as I headed for the bathroom. I locked myself in, took a Zanex and sat in the corner. I buried my face in my hands and sobbed.

How could it be that this monster who stole my entire world in mere hours, stood on the threshold of freedom while I would be a prisoner forever? I thought of him out there, free in my community. I could meet him at the bank, or the grocery store, what would I do? Respect his right to walk this earth a free man? No! No! No...

Brad banged on the door and snapped me out of my fear-induced trance, "Maddie! Are you okay?"

His question resonated with me for a moment, and I knew the answer, "No. I'm not okay."

"Open the door!" He knocked harder and I opened the door, "I'll never be okay," I confessed. My tear stained face made it clear I'd been crying.

"How many pills did you take?" he asked as he rummaged through my travel bag.

"I took one," I said.

Alex had left at some point and I felt bad for not having said goodbye, but I'm sure the atmosphere his descriptions of Twin Rivers had created was cause for him to take leave in quick form. Brad confiscated the Zanex, which wasn't necessary, if I'd wanted to do myself in I would have jumped when given the chance.

"If he gets out, I'm not sure I want to be here," I confessed. My honesty was a hard swallow for the both of us.

Brad guided me to the bed, "Let's get some sleep," he said. "Don't worry about this tonight."

I slid under the sheets and Brad's arms wrapped me in a shield of comfort. Miraculously, I slept.

The following morning Brad told me I'd had the worst nightmare he'd ever seen me have.

"I thought I'd have to do CPR," he said. He'd laid awake for the rest of the night, just watching me.

"I just wanted to make sure you didn't have another nightmare," he said.

What Brad didn't understand was that I was still living one.

CHAPTER 27 – CRAVING JUSTICE

"There may be times when we are powerless to prevent injustice, but there must never be a time when we fail to protest."

~Elle Wiesel

The following week I contacted Darrell Glover, a reporter from the Seattle Post-Intelligencer. We met at a local restaurant and I told him of my concern that, while I was in the Victim/Witness Notification Program and therefore had been promised to be notified of any movements by Chesnutt during his incarceration, I had not been told of his move to Twin Rivers some three months earlier.

"No one seems to be watching out for the victims," I said. "I think this needs to be looked into." Darrell agreed and said he'd look into it further and contact be the following week.

I contacted the Twin Rivers Correctional Center two days before "Hard Copy" was to air and advised the warden that she might not want to miss my segment.

"One of your inmates will be mentioned and I think you'll agree that he doesn't belong at Twin Rivers. He should be sent back to Walla Walla and if something isn't done, I'm going to the newspapers about this." I knew the power of bad press and I knew there had been enough publicity about the case to warrant attention—attention Twin Rivers and its chief administrators might find less than welcome.

I was pleased with the "Hard Copy" segment, which concentrated largely on Chesnutt and my role in capturing him. I decided that there was no time like the present to get the discussion going on the lack of attention to detail by the Victim/Witness Notification Program, and joined forces with Darrell Glover to get the story out.

I wrote letters. Lots of letters—demanding answers. Twin Rivers, the Victim/Witness Protection Program, the Secretary of the Department of Corrections;. "Who made the decision to transfer Allan Ray Chesnutt to Twin Rivers?"

"Why was I not notified of the transfer of Allan Chesnutt, and what steps can I take to ensure he's returned to Walla Walla State Penitentiary?" The more I wrote, the angrier I became that Chesnutt's "rights" were held in higher regard than my own.

I requested paperwork that stated he was not eligible for parole, I requested names of those who allowed him to slip through the cracks of the system, I compared him to Charles Campbell, a serial rapist who was allowed into a work release program and returned to, not only rape and kill his victim from eight years before, but her eight-year-old daughter and a neighbor as well. All three were dead due to a flawed system and I was determined that I would not be a fourth example of the state's lack of attention to detail.

A week after "Hard Copy" had aired, Darrell Glover called to tell me that his investigation into the story had revealed that Chesnutt had requested to be put into a sex offender's program. One that served to rehabilitate and that once he was determined to be eligible due to good behavior and transferred to Twin Rivers, he refused to take part in the program. But that wasn't all, there was good news,

"Five days after "Hard Copy" aired, Chesnutt was transferred back to Walla Walla," Darrell said. I felt my heart leap with whatever joy it could muster.

"This is no coincidence," I said.

"Probably not," said Darrell, "but I think our work is done. If anything changes, we'll fire up this story again," he promised. "In the meantime, rest easy."

I thanked him and quietly celebrated the fact that Chesnutt was once again at a safe distance, although I shuddered to think of what could have been had he slipped further through the cracks and been released. Would he have come back? After all, it was me who sabotaged his plan of attack on local women. It was me who turned the tables and morphed a terrorizing rapist into a criminal in chains and an orange jumpsuit. Would he have been a seeker of revenge?

On May 8th, 1996, I received a sole response to all the letters I had sent, it stated that Chesnutt's transfer to Twin Rivers was considered and approved for reasons of staffing and public safety. His initial agreement to take part in a rehabilitation program made him a good candidate for the transfer—according to them. Until he refused.

Allan Ray Chesnutt was transferred without my knowledge and that was not okay. Having enrolled in the Victim/Witness Program, I was told that I would be advised of any movement, escape from custody or subsequent capture. I was not and I was finding that less than acceptable.

The following day I drove to Everett to the Snohomish County Courthouse and requested all files on Allan Ray Chesnutt. I made copies of everything the files contained, then drove to my friend Mary Jane's to go over the records. Nowhere was it stated what the judge ordered on the day of sentencing, "No possibility of parole."

I was aware of a new law in Washington that stated, "Three strikes and you're out!" This meant that after a third conviction the felon is imprisoned for life. The law had been put into effect a month or two prior to Chesnutt's sentencing. I was hopeful that he had earned more than three strikes with the multiple rapes and assaults, but I was disappointed to learn that all his rape charges had been lumped together. The monster still had two more strikes.

My next session with Dr. Jantz would have us both questioning the reliability of the Department of Corrections and he advised me to check in with them every two months to track Chesnutt's whereabouts. He told me I was taking less of the "victim's" role by taking control of the situation and I did feel somewhat empowered in my ability to influence his incarceration.

It was true. Many times after the attack I believed there was nothing I could do to change things, I just allowed them to happen. I allowed myself to be victimized which kept me immersed in a victim mentality; helpless, needy and vulnerable. I felt stronger now,

I could recognize situations where someone was attempting to take advantage of me and I began to put up a fight.

I continued to check up on Chesnutt and my research led me to a prior conviction in Pierce County, I discovered that in August of 1992, less than a year before his attack on me, Chesnutt had raped an eighteen-year old girl. She had just graduated high school and was planning to embark on college life in just a few weeks. Chesnutt had entered her home through a bathroom window while she slept in her bed. He put a pillowcase over her head and raped her while threatening to kill her.

I read a statement from the girl that said she was unable to attend college as planned due to the attack and it would be more than two years after the attack that she would attempt to reclaim her life. It was after this rape that Chesnutt would relocate to the Lynnwood/Edmonds area to continue his crime spree.

It was only after his convictions for the Edmonds/Lynwood rapes that he would be charged with the Pierce County rape. His DNA was a match for the assailant and on June 13, 1995, Chesnutt was taken from Walla Walla Penitentiary to the Pierce County Courthouse where he was arraigned. He boldly entered a plea of "not guilty."

The evidence proved overwhelming and on January 26th, 1996, just two weeks shy of his trial date of February 14th, Chesnutt changed his plea to guilty. He was sentenced to 280 months for first degree rape and an additional 116 months for burglary. Both convictions would be lumped in with the Lynnwood/Edmonds serial rapes and the sentences would run concurrently.

He won a plea bargain and wouldn't get a second strike against him, nor would he be made to serve out the sentence after his sentence for the crimes in Snohamish County. According to court records, Chesnutt was taken to Monroe State Reformatory and Twin Rivers Correctional Center on January 26, 1996. He had just been found guilty of yet another rape, but was taken to, at best, a medium security facility.

I was convinced The Department of Corrections had their heads buried in the sand.

CHAPTER 28 – THE TRUE COLORS OF BRAD

"Don't say you miss me when it's your fault I'm gone."
~Lifequotesru

Brad's and mine on again, off again relationship was anything but stable and my nagging instincts told me it was anything but normal and healthy, as well. Our pattern of breaking up and getting back together, harsh words one minute and the silent treatment the next—I was a little disappointed in myself for going back for more. I knew my friends were.

Linda's name would continue to come up and ultimately lead to a fight. I often wondered if Brad relied on that to buy a few days of freedom to see his lady "friends" while I cooled my heels and retreated to Mary Jane's. After a blow-up, a few days would pass and he'd beg me to come back. I was beginning to care less and less about the relationship and I was growing tired of Brad's narcissism and lack of investment in me as someone he wished to grow old with.

The reconciliations would be blissful for a day or two, I'd think to myself, Maybe this time he means what he says. Maybe he really does want to spend the rest of his life with me—maybe this time it will be good. I'd end up returning for a few days, only to realize that this was how Brad controlled the relationship, he had a way with words when he wanted his way. He'd remind me of all the good times we'd shared and how there was so much more to come.

Then the other shoe would drop—and I'd be gone again, granting him a respite from our relationship. It was becoming a common theme.

Three weeks after the Montel William's show, Geraldo Rivera's producer contacted me. They wanted to fly me to New York to do the show. I was at Brad's when I took the call and he was there, but asleep. He'd been up all night restoring power after an outage from a windstorm that had swept through the northwest.

The producer told me they wanted to book flights within the next two hours and, while they okayed a travel companion, they had to know who it would be. I was feeling rushed, but under the circumstances I assumed it was because they wanted a guest with a traumatic story to have locked-in travel arrangements before they changed their mind.

I went upstairs and nudged Brad awake, "I'm sorry to wake you," I said, "but the Geraldo show called and they want me to come to New York. Will you come with me? They have to know within the hour."

He was less than thrilled that I had woken him, "You woke me to tell me that?!" he flipped on his side, obviously annoyed, "You tell them if they can't give you more time than that, then forget it. You're not going!" I left him to sleep, hoping he would wake in a better mood.

I assumed his lack of enthusiasm for a trip to New York was as good as a, "no", and I called Michelle. She said, "Yes!" before I could get the entire sentence out. I looked forward to another few days in the big city with my daughter. I called the producer and told them that Michelle would be accompanying me.

Two hours later, Brad appeared.

"Did you tell them to forget it?" he asked.

"I'm sorry for waking you," I said, "but they needed to have a name of the person who would be traveling with me. They had to book the flights."

"I'll go," he said.

I stiffened at the request, "I'm sorry, I already asked Michelle. I'm afraid it's too late."

"Call them back!" he demanded, "Tell them I'm going."

"I can't do that," I countered. "Michelle's already looking forward to going."

He began to get angry and I took leave to pack before it escalated into something unpleasant—the way it always did.

* * * *

We boarded the plane and it was mother/daughter time again. Michelle had been trying to get pregnant and it was at 30,000 feet that she would share her good news. I was going to be a grandmother again and Evan was going to be a big brother! She asked that I keep it a secret until they were ready to announce, I gave her my word.

The Geraldo Rivera Show wanted to begin the show with my 911 call and me, this time I relented and agreed to go first. I told Michelle I wouldn't search for her face in the crowd this time and we weren't going to cry. He wasn't as personable as Montel and even pronounced my name wrong, until a production assistant corrected him during a break.

The whole experience lasted less than twenty minutes and both Michelle and I were glad when we were able to leave the studio, head to the hotel and just enjoy the city. The show aired on February 20th, 1996.

When we returned to Washington, I stayed at Brad's and he let me know I had another nightmare. "I don't think these shows are doing you any good," he said.

"I get that, but Dr. Jantz feels it's good for me. I'm helping other victims and their families," I stressed that any positive from that treacherous night should be soaked up.

"I disagree," he said. His lack of support was becoming more and more evident. We had a breakup right before my birthday toward the end of March of 1996. This one would last five days and when the eventual reconcile happened, he asked about my birthday, but didn't make any gesture to celebrate it.

Consistent with our pattern, we broke up again a few days before Brad's birthday. I recalled how hurt I had been that the person who claimed to love me, made no move to celebrate my own birthday and as much as I wanted to buy him a gift, or at the very least, a card when his birthday came around in late April, I decided I'd give him a taste of his own thoughtless medicine.

And did nothing.

He called and asked me to come over, it was the day after his birthday and while I felt a little guilty for disregarding it, I was determined to let him know how it felt to be forgotten. I secretly wanted him to feel he pain I felt the month before.

When I went over to his place, he acted sad and told me he celebrated alone with his children.

"Things need to change, Brad," I said. "It's not always about you and your feelings, sometimes, it's about me." I felt empowered to express my true feelings—whether I was reaching him or not, was a whole other story.

* * * *

Brad had physical problems, he'd had back surgery two years earlier and the result was that his right side would experience profound numbness. Heart problems, hyperthyroidism, the need for Coumadin in his diet to prevent stroke; he was aware of every ache and pain and would be sure that I was aware as well.

He'd request back rubs and foot massages to ward off aches and pains, but would rarely reciprocate, if at all. He smoked and drank way too much and although his job required a fair amount of physical exertion, he didn't exercise. At forty-one years old, I wondered if he would live to see his children grow up.

One of the largest aerospace companies in the world had begun offering assessment tests for employment and I signed up for the 4 ½ hour test. It was a total of seven parts and all seven parts had to be passed in order to be considered for employment. It was difficult, but I passed all seven parts and was advised I was a likely candidate.

I was proud of my accomplishment, but when I shared it with Brad he was less than thrilled—once again.

"I don't want you working around all those men," he said.

"If I get an offer, I'm taking it," I said. "It's a great opportunity." I was growing weary of Brad's attempt to keep me under his thumb when he wanted to be together, and pick a fight when he wanted time away. He didn't like or accept any of my male friends, but I was expected to accept the fact that he carried a list of his female friends and their numbers at the ready. Something just didn't feel right.

My acing the test proved intimidating for him and he was determined to take me down a notch—or two, when given the chance. What I craved was a partner who lifted me up, saw the best in me and wanted nothing more than to nourish that. Brad was intent on squelching anything that threatened to boost my confidence. If I remained the needy victim, then he had control.

* * * *

The interviews continued. Ladies Home Journal joined the band-wagon of publications interested in telling my story. The more interviews I did, the more I was determined that rape and Allan Chesnutt would not define me. The one-page article was to come out in the Fall of '96.

Celebrity that arises out of violence is never pleasant. The victim is forever reminded of the incident that catapulted them into the limelight. I would be happily going about my day; the attack shoved neatly into the back of my mind, when the phone would ring,

"Ms. Morehouse? We'd like to interview you...", and BAM—I would be back in the bedroom of the townhome, my head against the sideboard—my world instantly altered. I would have preferred anonymity and the calm of a life un-assaulted, but I was determined to turn the enormous negative into something positive and national outlets that might lead to helping another victim of violent crime was one way to do it.

While Brad saw the media spotlight to be a trigger for nightmares and a hurdle toward healing, I saw it as a way to give the unthinkable experience purpose. More than 150,000 rapes occur each year—150,000! That's more than 400 rapes and sexual assaults per day and those are the ones that are reported. No one knows how many go unreported and I felt my story might help victims understand, "It's not your fault. It's not your fault—it's not your fault."

Brad had a difficult time grasping the concept of helping others; the strength I gained by reaching out was powerful and I knew I was getting better. By attempting to keep me in a place of pain and resign, he only served to make me aware of where I didn't belong.

I didn't belong in a place that pushed me down. I was determined to get up.

CHAPTER 29 – THE DARK BEFORE THE DAWN

"It is health that is real wealth, not pieces of gold and silver."
~Mahatma Gandhi

The lump was undeniable. I called to make an appointment with my doctor and explained my findings. They asked that I come in that morning.

The doctor asked when I'd had my last mammogram and I had to be honest, "It's been at least four or five years," I confessed. "I've just been so busy."

I hated visits to the doctor or dentist where you felt compelled to explain why you'd taken a reprieve from your responsibilities to your own health. I had always been relieved to get the good news, "Everything looks just fine, but please make sure you make those regular appointments."

Not this time—this time they found lumps in both breasts and seemed more concerned about the breast I hadn't come in to have checked. "There's a significant lump in the other breast and we'd like to address that as soon as possible." I was scheduled to see a surgeon the next day.

I returned to Brad's and was met with the usual questions, "Where were you all day?" I told him I'd been to the doctor, but it was clear he was concerned that the laundry had piled up.

"I'm seeing the surgeon tomorrow," I said.

He took me in his arms and said, "It's going to be okay." The next words out of his mouth were to tell me he'd be spending the evening with a friend who was helping him restore an old car.

"I won't be late," he said. "We'll watch a movie when I get back."

I wanted him to stay with me, but I was reluctant to start an argument. I thought about all the times I had seen him through doctor visits and diagnosis, but he seemed incapable of giving back. I no longer took his actions personally. Brad was Brad and I learned to numb my response to his lack of compassion. He returned late that night and smelling of alcohol, climbed into bed and fell asleep instantly. I laid awake, wishing the unwelcome lumps away—hoping I'd get one more reprieve, one more, "Everything looks fine."

* * * *

"There are five suspicious lumps," the doctor said. I struggled to concentrate as he spoke. "They are hard and don't appear to be calcium deposits or fibroid—if it's determined to be cancer then I feel we've caught it in time to remove them and take the necessary measures. We'll do conventional treatments to ensure we get it all."

"Conventional treatments? What do you mean?" I was trying desperately to understand what was happening to my body.

"Chemotherapy and radiation," he said matter-of-factly. "I'll schedule surgery for the end of the week."

The doctor asked if someone could be with me the day of surgery and I assured him there would be. "You can't drive after the procedure," he advised.

I knew he was right and promised that I would have someone with me. Who that someone would be, I didn't yet know.

"Do you want me to take you?" Brad asked.

I was uncomfortable and not even sure I meant what I was saying, I just wanted someone to care about my plight as much as I did. "That would be nice," I said.

"I'll try to get off work," he said. I knew Brad could get off work if he wanted to. He had taken many last minute days off to float in the pool or recover from a hangover, as a result of one of our break-ups. I was hurt that he didn't find this occasion worthy of a sick or vacation day.

The following evening, I asked, "Will you be able to take me tomorrow?" His mood shifted, "I really need the money," he said. "I don't know how you think I can just drop everything. I have a job...just because you don't—" I couldn't believe what I was hearing.

Brad was well aware that I had my own money, but since the day he'd helped me move the Caffé Aida supplies into storage, he'd been after me to re-open my business. He'd constantly mention a lot down the street from his house.

"I fell in love with the lady who owned the expresso shop," he'd say. "What happened to her?"

I hadn't changed, but he'd continue to attempt to manipulate me with hurtful words. His attacks would only make me more intent in not re-opening, I realized I didn't want to be so close to his house. With our sporadic, on-again-off-again pattern, I didn't want to see his house during our breaks, I feared I might see something hurtful.

Brad and I didn't speak during dinner, a little later he relented with, "If you really want me to take you, I guess I can." I felt like a burden and probably should have declined his offer, but instead I said, "I would appreciate it, after all, I've accompanied you to all your appointments and they weren't even surgical—he became agitated and cut me off, "Just shut up!" he snapped, "I'll take you!"

I was confused, I couldn't understand why I allowed him to speak to me that way. Mutual respect was something Tom and I had never strayed from during our marriage, and yet I was settling for so much less with Brad. I knew I deserved better, but I'd constantly return for more punishment. I went to bed early without uttering a word in return.

The next morning Brad acted put out during the drive to the medical center. Traffic was light and we arrived early. Once we checked in with the receptionist, we waited in chairs. Brad read the paper, but soon became fidgety, "Maybe you should find out how much longer it's going to be."

"They know we're here," I said, "I'm sure it won't be much longer." I hesitated before adding, "Thank you for taking me." His response was a slightly audible, "Yeah."

When the nurse called my name, she asked Brad if he would be waiting for me, his response was much kinder to the nurse, "I'll be right here," he said with a smile.

The procedure was painful, they ran fine wires to the lumps in my breasts and it was barely tolerable—once they were in place the intense stinging ceased. The nurse brought me back to where Brad was waiting and directed us to the outpatient area of the hospital.

Once inside my room, I was instructed to change into a gown and get into bed. Brad went back to reading his paper in the chair next to the bed. The nurse returned and told me what to expect during the procedure. She inserted a needle into my wrist and started an IV. While Brad was friendly with the nurse, as soon as she left he'd return to his paper, making it crystal clear that he didn't want to be there with me. I felt more alone than if he wasn't there at all.

I was scared—cancer was unthinkable after all I'd been through over the past three years. I didn't want any more pain. My eyes welled at the thought of bad news.

When the nurse came in to check on me, tears were trickling down my face. Brad continued to read his paper, oblivious to my fears. The nurse took my hand, "We're going to take very good care of you," she said. "What can I get you?"

I glanced toward Brad, "It would be nice if he could just hold my hand," I said. The nurse looked at Brad; she shook her head in disgust, "Would you please hold her hand?" Her tone was sharp and Brad quickly complied.

The nurse left the room and Brad snapped, "I can't believe you said that!" He was fuming and although he continued to hold my hand, he wouldn't look at me and didn't say another word.

When I woke from surgery I was sore and nauseous. Brad was still in the room; I was almost surprised he was still there. The nurse helped me get dressed and gently explained that my doctor should have the pathology report sometime the following week.

Back at Brad's house, he helped me inside. He led me to the couch and covered me with a blanket, his kinder side had returned.

"I'll pick up your prescriptions and be right back," he said.

I dozed until his return and took the pain medication the doctor had prescribed; within a short time, I was sick to my stomach. Brad helped me to the bathroom and I threw-up. The pain was bad, but the nausea was worse. I continued to throw up at least once an hour, my abdominal muscles ached from retching.

Brad handled the incoming calls from friends and family and I briefly spoke to Michelle, letting her know I'd be up for a visit the following day. I wanted to see them. I wanted to feel better.

Brad went out for fast food and when he returned I was bent over the toilet, heaving again. A call to my doctor would determine that it was probably the pain pills and that I should switch to plain Tylenol instead.

Soon the vomiting subsided and Brad prepared some soup for me. He sat beside me on the couch as I sipped the clear broth.

"I can't believe how you embarrassed me in front of that nurse!" he said. "How do you think that made me feel, Maddie? Huh? How do you think that made me feel?" His tone of voice increased with each word.

I came to my own defense, "I just wanted you to hold my hand. I was scared, why couldn't you see that?"

"I can't believe you," he growled. I was in no mood for an argument, I hurt and was weak from all the vomiting.

"I'm going to bed," he said. "Are you going to stay down here?" I almost wanted to say "yes" but in my weakened state, I knew I'd feel safer in bed, next to Brad. Even if he was angry again.

He helped me up the stairs and into bed, when I woke the next morning he was already up. I could hear him on the phone making plans with his friend. He barely said good morning.

"What are you doing today?" he asked.

"Not much, Michelle and Jake are bringing Evan around noon," I answered as I poured coffee into a mug. I was still sore and any movement was a reminder of my surgery.

"I'm headed out—working on the car today," he said. He made no effort to ask how I was feeling, and it was clear he had no plans to stick around to see the kids. I knew at that moment that I needed to escape the roller coaster I had been riding with Brad. I had finally had enough of his cruel words and actions.

I knew he'd never change—he didn't want to change. I was tired of worrying about sexually transmitted diseases after we'd reconcile after a break-up. While I wasn't seeing anyone during our time apart, I was well aware that he was out drinking with "lady friends". When I'd ask about those transgressions, he'd simply say, "We were broke up."

As sore and uncomfortable as I was, I suddenly knew I deserved much more. Perhaps I had been putting up with the harsh words and emotional abuse because, having been a victim of both Chesnutt and Ted; having lost my business to red tape and bureaucracy, I had grown accustomed to being the prey. I had fallen into the role and was lodged in a crevice of sacrifice. I had surrendered my self-worth, my ideals and my expectations of what life had in store for me.

I thought of my sister-in-law, Mary Jane, and her question to me, "Why do you keep going back for more?" I'd never have a good answer and she'd always respond with, "I respect your right to be wrong."

I thought about Cassie Haden and all the girls I had counseled after their own experience of being victim. I thought of all the times I told them they shouldn't allow their attacker to define them as less deserving because of the experience. I thought of all the times I told them they were worth the effort to heal and grow past the crime that was committed against them and rise from the ashes.

I was instantly enlightened that I hadn't practiced what I had preached to all those women—and men. I had allowed myself to stay in one place; to root myself in that horrific night in May three year earlier. I had allowed fear to engulf me and in that process, I had forgotten to truly enjoy my life.

Maybe it was the combination of Brad's insensitivity and the threat of cancer, but I was determined to face whatever lay before me with the determination and faith I'd been known for all my life. I was done being the victim.

As soon as Brad left I began gathering the few things I kept there, I planned to leave his house before he returned. I packed my car and waited for Michelle and Jake to arrive with Evan. As soon as they entered I told them I was leaving; I'd had enough.

"We've heard this before," said Jake.

"This time it's different," I said with conviction. "This time the one worth saving—is me."

EPILOGUE

I prayed every day that I didn't have breast cancer, more than a week had passed and I hadn't heard from my doctor. The uncertainty was almost as bad as the surgery itself, but I came to terms with it. If I had cancer, I would beat that, too. I felt energized and ready to emerge into the rest of my life—my optimism as to what that would hold was strong and that was something I hadn't felt in a very long time.

Brad called a few times in an effort to convince me to return, but I was firm in my decision that our relationship was over. Once in a while I'd get lonely and think of him, but quickly remind myself of how the unpleasant memories of Brad and I far outweighed the good.

A week and five days after my surgery the doctor's office called with the news; my prayers had been answered. Benign. I didn't have cancer.

The nurse apologized for taking so long to get back to me, but the doctor was so convinced it was cancer that when the test returned negative, he sent it up to be retested, only to have it return as negative a second time. I thanked her profusely and immediately called Michelle and Jeffery with the good news.

My children. My greatest gift—they saw me through my darkest days. I think back on the days in which I was immersed in confusion and hopelessness. They held me up and never once gave up on encouraging me to emerge from the aftermath of Allan Chesnutt and his brutality. They also instinctively knew when I was to start doing for myself once more.

I had never been a reckless person, as a rape counselor, I had heard the stories of women who hitchhiked, or drank too much at parties and ended up in a back room with an aggressor—I probably passed judgment on them more than I care to admit; I surmised that a violent attack would never happen to me—I was far too careful.

I was raped in my own bedroom, in a locked townhome. I understand now that what happened to me could happen to anyone, regardless of how "careful" they are. I realize that I can tiptoe through my life looking over my shoulder for the next violent act; one that would catapult me right back into the role of helpless, confused and traumatized victim, but to do so would cap my quality of life—it would be me that was the culprit, robbing myself of opportunity, laughter and love.

I had a degree of Post-Traumatic Stress Syndrome. I'd slip into moments of fear and regret, and Dr. Jantz said that was perfectly normal for someone who had experienced a life threatening situation. I learned to allow those feelings to be present for a time, but I'd soon send them on their way by simply accepting them for what they were, giving them little power over me.

I had to push past my aversion to strange men, no matter what their age. A strange man was a threatening one and once I became aware of my tendency to back away, I would work hard to make and maintain eye contact. Once I mastered that, the threat all but disappeared.

Three of my closest friends happen to be men, so I know my experience didn't affect my ability to enjoy relationships, I just became better at choosing the right people to spend my time with.

I have regained my faith in the idea that most men are caring, kind and loving individuals. By choosing to focus on that, I rob those like Chesnutt of any power. While I do enjoy falling in love, I don't need a relationship to feel complete, I've learned that I would rather be alone than in an unhealthy relationship.

Dr. Jantz helped me to accept my parents' and sister's response to the attack. Reactions such as theirs were not uncommon. Being cast in the limelight due to something as traumatic (and to them, shameful) as rape was impossible for them to tolerate.

I was sorry when they declined to attend the Medal of Valor ceremony, I felt that they would have been proud to be my parents. I also felt that maybe they would have grasped a better understanding of the magnitude of what had occurred. I now understand that they were probably suffering from shock and having

lived a relatively quiet life, their own trauma from the episode was foreign and paralyzing.

The pain they likely felt was overwhelming and that was something I had to come to terms with. My love for them never wavered, as I know they loved me until their last day on Earth—and beyond.

Several years after the attack my mother admitted her anger to me, saying she didn't know how to help. We continued to heal with family gatherings and celebrations and found comfort in the company of one another.

I was eventually offered the job with the aerospace company whose test I had aced months earlier. I enjoyed years of of employment there and made some wonderful friends that became my extended family. To top that off, Michelle gave birth to a daughter and I was thoroughly enjoying my role as grandmother to Evan and MacKenzie.

I learned to accept the support of others. An extended hand or a willing ear were instrumental in my gaining the ability to fully trust again. I learned the value in allowing family, friends, co-workers, counselors and support groups to reach out and encourage those in crisis.

It was two years after the attack, when I'd heard that Ted had sold the house and moved to another state, that I felt safe enough to sleep without my gun at arm's length. I relied solely on Chanel to alert me to any out of the ordinary noise and if necessary, I knew I could get to my gun before anyone got to me.

My experience with the media played a positive in helping me to see things in perspective. The emotional baggage I was able to shed on national television empowered me in that I was an example of how, with the proper help, one could heal. I made it clear that while Chesnutt's attack on me took mere hours, the result was years of work to become whole again. I hoped that by sharing my own experience, I had encouraged others to get on the road to recovery.

My final act of reclaiming my life was writing this book, I was able to recall each event with crystal clear clarity and by facing the good, the bad and the ugly, I am able to see my life in a whole new light. As I wrote, I felt my fears melt away. With each page I was able to shed some of the anger that plagued me as a result of the crime.

Shortly after the attack I was given the option to change my name for reasons of security and personal safety. I considered it, but then realized that I would be giving Chesnutt even more power over me. By altering my identity, he would have accomplished what he had initially threatened; removing me from the face of the earth. I decided he would never claim that victory.

I continue to check on Chesnutt's confinement, not out of paranoia, but out of my responsibility to myself and other potential victims. The last time I checked I was told he would be confined until 2058. That works for me, as he'll be eighty-five years old—if he makes it that long.

I trust my instincts now; I'm not easily persuaded by others. If something doesn't feel right, I step away. If my gut tells me a particular person might be a threat to my wellbeing, I don't get involved.

My friends are my stronghold. Michelle and Jeffery are my rock. My (now) five grandchildren are my joy and my life is good again, I look forward to what each day holds.

I am happy. I am healthy and I've come a long way from that night in May of 1993.

I have triumphed over adversity—and I do believe in miracles.

lived a relatively quiet life, their own trauma from the episode was foreign and paralyzing.

The pain they likely felt was overwhelming and that was something I had to come to terms with. My love for them never wavered, as I know they loved me until their last day on Earth—and beyond.

Several years after the attack my mother admitted her anger to me, saying she didn't know how to help. We continued to heal with family gatherings and celebrations and found comfort in the company of one another.

I was eventually offered the job with the aerospace company whose test I had aced months earlier. I enjoyed years of of employment there and made some wonderful friends that became my extended family. To top that off, Michelle gave birth to a daughter and I was thoroughly enjoying my role as grandmother to Evan and MacKenzie.

I learned to accept the support of others. An extended hand or a willing ear were instrumental in my gaining the ability to fully trust again. I learned the value in allowing family, friends, co-workers, counselors and support groups to reach out and encourage those in crisis.

It was two years after the attack, when I'd heard that Ted had sold the house and moved to another state, that I felt safe enough to sleep without my gun at arm's length. I relied solely on Chanel to alert me to any out of the ordinary noise and if necessary, I knew I could get to my gun before anyone got to me.

My experience with the media played a positive in helping me to see things in perspective. The emotional baggage I was able to shed on national television empowered me in that I was an example of how, with the proper help, one could heal. I made it clear that while Chesnutt's attack on me took mere hours, the result was years of work to become whole again. I hoped that by sharing my own experience, I had encouraged others to get on the road to recovery.

My final act of reclaiming my life was writing this book, I was able to recall each event with crystal clear clarity and by facing the good, the bad and the ugly, I am able to see my life in a whole new light. As I wrote, I felt my fears melt away. With each page I was able to shed some of the anger that plagued me as a result of the crime.

Shortly after the attack I was given the option to change my name for reasons of security and personal safety. I considered it, but then realized that I would be giving Chesnutt even more power over me. By altering my identity, he would have accomplished what he had initially threatened; removing me from the face of the earth. I decided he would never claim that victory.

I continue to check on Chesnutt's confinement, not out of paranoia, but out of my responsibility to myself and other potential victims. The last time I checked I was told he would be confined until 2058. That works for me, as he'll be eighty-five years old—if he makes it that long.

I trust my instincts now; I'm not easily persuaded by others. If something doesn't feel right, I step away. If my gut tells me a particular person might be a threat to my wellbeing, I don't get involved.

My friends are my stronghold. Michelle and Jeffery are my rock. My (now) five grandchildren are my joy and my life is good again, I look forward to what each day holds.

I am happy. I am healthy and I've come a long way from that night in May of 1993.

I have triumphed over adversity—and I do believe in miracles.

Made in the USA
Charleston, SC
14 June 2016